Wicca Starter Kit

A Step by Step Guide for the Solitary Practitioner to Learn the Use of Fundamental Elements of Wiccan Rituals Such as Candles, Herbs, Tarot, Crystals and Spells

By: Joy Cunningham

Table of Contents

Introduction

Wicca Starter Kit is your ultimate guide to casting spells and performing rituals with all of the tools you will need to bring the power of nature and the divine into your life. When you are a solitary practitioner, you are in charge of the rituals, the tools that you will use and the types of spells that you want to create to perform your magical rites. Finding all of the right tools can be a challenge and having a great resource guide to help you get started can make all the difference.

Whether or not you are new to Wicca, or have been practicing for a short while, this book will give you an overview and introduction to the history of Wicca, the concepts behind its philosophies and some of the reasons for celebration of this beautiful magic. It is important to have the background to understand the tools and reasons for your practice.

The most important part of Wicca Starter Kit is your guide to the tools you will need to perform your rituals and spells. In chapter 2, you will find a concise list of magical implements to help you explore your Wicca practice and will give you an understanding of what they are used for, how to use them, when to use them, and where you can find them for your altar and practice.

Wicca Starter Kit will also provide you with several chapters of step-by-step instructions for building and honoring your altar space, casting a magic circle, performing rituals and writing and casting spells. You will also find a chapter dedicated to the use of crystal magic as well as one devoted to candle magic.

Overall, Wicca Starter Kit is a great guide to help you in your journey with rituals and spells through the use of some of the most common tools of the trade. Whatever you find here in these pages, it is sure to expand your knowledge of your craft and help you get further on your path of practicing Wiccan magic.

So mote it be!

Chapter 1: Introduction to Wicca

Wicca: A Brief History

Welcome to a brief history of Wicca! As you become acquainted with the mysteries and magic of this beautiful craft, it will be important for you to have an idea of where it has derived from. Many of the traditions of Wicca come from more ancient Pagan belief systems and practices, however the advent of Wicca and its founding philosophies originated in England and was introduced in the mid 1950's by a British civil servant by the name of Gerald Gardner.

A basic idea of Wicca is that it is considered what some might term Neo-Paganism, however there are distinct qualities and characteristics that set it apart from the traditional denominations of the paganism practiced in more ancient cultures.

Prior to Gardner's introduction of Wicca to the public in 1954, the concepts of Wicca could be traced back to a woman named Margaret Murray who was a renowned folklorist, anthropologist and Egyptologist, who studied the traditions and cultures of a wide range of religious practices, combining a field study of these sects and describing in her own words the concept of witchcraft.

Murray wrote a large set of books about medieval religious practices, specifically those centered on witch-cults in Europe. Her works actually inspired readers to rekindle the pagan arts by creating their own covens, structuring their worship around the descriptions from Murray's books. All of this was going on in the early 1920's in Great Britain and Europe and likely led to Gerald Gardner's more structured philosophy called Wicca.

Gardener's book entitled *Witchcraft Today* demonstrated the origin of the word Wicca and what it means to the craft. In his book, it is actually spelled with only one 'c', as in "wica", and it wasn't until the 1960's that the second 'c' was added. Gardner mentions that the word 'wica' is a Gaelic, or Scots-English word meaning "wise people". He had always had an interest in the occult and eventually became initiated into a coven of his own in the late 1930's.

Eventually, he formed his own coven in the late 40's, buying land and establishing it as a center for the study of folklore. It became his occult headquarters and where he would bring to light the Wiccan way through his writing and practice.

A great connection existed between Gardner and the famed occultist Aleister Crowley. The two men met in the late 1940's and had much to discuss about their personal beliefs and magic. Gardner's work and writing out of his own rituals of Wicca for publication were strongly influenced by Crowley's own work, which had dated all the way back to the earlier part of the century.

Gardner published his works, one of them being a novel entitled, *High Magic's Aid*, which actually became one of his first standard tomes to describe the practice of Wicca. It was his *Book of Shadows*, however, that became the most highly regarded and sought after. Gardner's Book of Shadows was his personal collection of spells, rituals and other information about the craft. To this day, it is one of the most central books for the practice of Wicca, or at least for learning from the original Wiccan, Gardner himself. Fortunately, Wicca was then, and remains to be, an ever-evolving practice and does not adhere to a strict set of rules. It happens to be a very flexible religion and offers that people follow a simple set of ideas and concepts and that there is freedom within those ideas to explore and form a deeper understanding.

Initiates of Gardner's coven were given the Book of Shadows to copy out and use and that was one of the ways they belonged to the coven, sharing the same spells and rituals to carry forward and practice.

Gardner met Doreen Valiente in the early 1950's, before Wicca had its coming out. She personally contacted him after seeing an article in a magazine about covens, witches, their practices, and what that reality was like. Under Gardner's guidance, she was able to revise *The Book of Shadows* for Gardner to offer it as a popular book for others outside of the coven and also prominent Wiccan circles, similar to how Crowley had marketed his beliefs and findings. Valiente became a Wiccan leader of her own coven and was a prominent figure and scholar in the world of steadily growing Wiccans.

The story of Wicca, when you look at it like that, seems like no more than a trifle in the annals of history, but when you look a little deeper, it had a profound impact on the world of magic. Leading up to Gardner's exposure of his new religion, there were several ways that people were still looking to practice the ancient Pagan arts. Witchcraft was an incredibly taboo practice and it was highly frowned upon for centuries after the witch trials.

The study of the past by Margaret Murray helped people to find a new appreciation and understanding for the beauty of this magic and if it wasn't for her work, and that of other occult philosophers, Wicca might not have been born.

To be honest, it has always existed in some form or fashion and it has carried many other names. The big umbrella term for it would be Pagan, and that word houses a whole cornucopia of possible sects and denominations, practices and rituals.

So then, it begs the question: what makes Wicca different?

Based in nature worship of the pagan religions, modern-day Wicca approaches connection to the divine through rituals and practices, festivals of the solstices, observances of deities, specifically a male and female god form, herbalism, a code of ethics and a belief in reincarnation and an afterlife.

Some say that it is a modern-day interpretation of those pagan religions and traditions, which existed before Christianity. It has its origins in Europe, but in today's world will also incorporate concepts from other religious practices like Shamanism and pre-

Christian Egyptian religion. It has been noted that there are strong similarities to Druidism, as well, despite there being a lack of evidence about how the Druids truly worshipped.

A majority of Wiccans are duotheistic, meaning they worship a male god and a female goddess, or the Horned God and Mother Goddess, or Mother Earth. It is not always the case and even the early forms of Wicca, back in Gardner's day, were not strict. Most of the time, it was determined on a coven by coven basis, what deities would be worshiped by the group and how to perform certain rituals.

Some other forms of Wiccan practice involve, and are not limited to, atheism, pantheism, and polytheism. This opens the playing field to anyone wishing to establish a Wiccan practice, involving all of the other ethics and rituals into their work, while getting the chance to determine how they want to worship. The basics remain the same, but the deities or what gets worshipped changes.

Apart from these components outlined in the earliest forms of Wicca, there is a devout appreciation for the Earth and all of her inhabitants which is why Wicca tends to be called a nature-based religion. The use of herbs and plants in spell work and rituals is celebrated regularly, and also includes a devotion to the seasons of the Earth cycles and Moon cycles, bringing focus to all living rhythms.

The history of Wicca may feel recent; however, it comes from a long and green history of pagans, druids, witches, warlocks and all of the individuals and covens along the way who had a sincere devotion to the presence of Earth magic and all of its gifts. Giving attention to the origins of Wicca is an important beginning to your study and as you embrace the methods of how Wicca can be practiced, like those before you, you can build upon it to make it work for you the way that feels best. There are only guidelines and no strict rules. Wicca is meant to evolve with the individual, and whether you are practicing alone or in a group, the Wicca of the past will always be a part of the Wicca of the present. Your Wicca.

The next chapter will go deeper into some of the core beliefs and philosophies of all branches of Wicca to help you determine your own safe practice.

Wicca Core Beliefs and Philosophies

Wicca can be described as a broad religion as it has the happiness of including a lot of different perspectives, realities and beliefs. There are, however, several major core beliefs that are practiced by a majority of Wiccans as a way to establish a grounding basis for understanding the magic you are working with when you are practicing.

These concepts are taken into account, no matter what coven you are in, or what deity you are worshipping. The concepts outlined in this chapter are main platform, or foundation, of what Wicca is and how it explains itself to anyone wishing to follow this path.

Nature is Divine

A majority of Wiccans will tell you that nature is divine. It is like a backbone to the entire practice and there are so many ways that this core belief manifests itself in these rituals. We are all members of this Earth: every rock, tree, leaf, plant, animal, bird, insect, and person, not to mention hundreds of thousands of other species and landscapes.

The Earth is or sacred home and we are a sacred part of it. It is where all life energy is stored and recreated and we are a part of those cycles and systems. To worship nature is to worship the very essence of all things. And you will find that all Wiccan holidays and festivals that are celebrated are derived from a worship of nature. Each festival is marked by a solstice or equinox. All esbats are marked by the cycle of the moon. And just about every ingredient in the rituals and spells of these festivities comes from nature somehow.

There is also a celebration in nature of the unity of opposing forces. There is always a balance of the light and the dark and nature-worship provides the opportunity to look at life from that place of balance and serenity. It is the presence of the male and female in all things; the yin and the yang. That is nature.

The practice of devoting space and love to nature is a part of the Wiccan creed and even though it is not a demand that you follow that practice, it comes naturally when you consider all of the other core beliefs.

Many of the tools that you will use for your rituals and spells are derived from nature. You will find yourself gathering herbs or pieces of wood for making a wand. You may be harvesting certain plants to hang around your house for a certain holiday, or dressing your altar in the perfumes and trinkets of the forest floor. All of nature comes into Wicca and it is a powerful process to fully connect with the divine in nature.

Karma, The Afterlife and Reincarnation

Karma is an echo of what you may find in the Threefold Law (see below) which basically states that what you do in this life carries over into your next one. To make such a suggestion, one must believe in the concept of reincarnation, which creates an open doorway for your spiritual being and essence to return to another life, after your last one, to continue to learn lessons and acquire knowledge for the evolution of all things.

According to Wicca, this is what will always be and has always been, and so in order to adopt the principles of Wicca, you must look into the reality of who you were before, and who you are going to be next. It might be that you are already familiar with some of your past life experiences and you already know what lessons you are trying to learn from those lives. In other cases, for some, you gain new knowledge as you go and are not always privy to what you are supposed to be learning. The concept of

Karma asks that you remind yourself what you need to heal from your former lives so that you can ascend further into your true power and magic. And while you are at it, in this life you are living now, be sure that what you do is something you want to take with you into the next life. This also pertains to the Wiccan Rede 'harm none' (see below).

Although there is the concept of reincarnation, there is also the concept of the afterlife, sometimes referred to as Summerland, and it is here that you rest between lives to prepare for the next one, to gather your strength and reflect on the journey before to create the best journey forward.

All of these concepts help the Wiccan to bridge the gap between Earth and Spirit and that the balance of the divine is always present, no matter what life you are living, or what stage of travel you are in between worlds.

Ancestors

It is not uncommon to call upon the ancestors in the practice of Wiccan rituals and casting. Many Wiccans believe that our ancestors are always with us, guiding us and showing us the way and should be honored for their own commitment to forging ahead and living life.

Wiccans celebrate deities of various kinds and it is normal to include your ancestors in your practice just as frequently, as they are a part of the cycle of the self and have many lessons to teach as you grow and honor your own path. The concept of honoring the ancestors in not specific to Wicca and is a cross-cultural truth, present in most religious practices.

A great deal of worship for the ancestors comes from a need to embrace the past as well as what your ancestors continue to do for you in the future.

Wheel of the Year

All of the cycles of the year are celebrated in Wicca. Every solstice has a celebration, or Sabbat, and every equinox, too. The rituals and spells that accompany these times are a sacred honoring and celebration committed to the end of something to hail the beginning of something new. In the calendar of the year, there are endless deaths and rebirths that can occur and as a Wiccan, you will find harmony and abundance with every passing season because of that very truth: life begets death which begets more life.

In a all of the seasons there are also moon cycles that are celebrated throughout the ritual of Esbats. The cycles of the moon organize the seasons and every waning moon leads to an ending, into a darkening, while every waxing moon leads to a powerful fullness that has its own magic and ritual associated with it.

All of the rhythms and cycles are a part of Wiccan work and it will be a part of this world forever. The concept of worshiping the divine in nature goes closely with the wheel of the year and should be counted as a major component of Wiccan worship.

Personal Responsibility and Responsibility

This concept agrees with the Wiccan Rede and the Threefold Law. You are responsible for every action you take. Wicca asks that you are wise to your power because it might be more than you realize, especially when you are working with the sacred divine energies of all things and all life.

When you are practicing Wicca, you are becoming responsible for more than just yourself; you are using the energy of all life to celebrate and support the life you lead and everything you choose can have an impact on another. It is a wonderful way for you to be honest with the truth of karma as well, because whatever you are responsible for in this life, goes with you forward into the next.

You are incredibly powerful, and Wicca helps you to embrace your internal power and life force energy; it also asks you to be responsible with your power and to harm none and do right by your actions and rituals.

The Wiccan Rede: Harm None

The Wiccan Rede simply states that you should do nothing in your practice that could cause harm to another individual. The basic concept of the golden rule of thumb, that you would do unto others, but it is also asking you to be very cautious in your practice and to consider how you are wording your spells and rituals.

The practice of Wicca is meant to be of benefit to the greater good of all life and so a lot of it has to do with intentions. When you are practicing you might find that you need to state that you are wanting to harm none and that you will uphold the good of all living things on Earth, so it be in your power.

You will find this credo in all of the Wiccan books you find and it has held steady and true for some time. It holds you to your personal responsibility and power and that you have to be the one to make the right choice when using the gift of magic.

Equality

Coercion is not an element of the Wiccan faith. Proselytizing is frowned upon and an aura of acceptance for all backgrounds and spiritual purposes is embraced. Wiccans generally believe that there needs to be an equality in all matters and that all people have a right to walk their own spiritual path; the one that is right for them.

The concept of equality should go without saying in all religions, but unfortunately this is often not the case. This is one way that Wicca is so unique; it offers a way to receive wisdom and abundance through worship of the divine without suggesting that it can only be done a certain way.

Wicca equals equality and the practicing of this artful religion requires an open heart and an open mind to anyone who is in need of a spiritual community and path.

Rule of Three

The Threefold Law, aka Rule of Three, is used in many Wiccan traditions. Not everyone supports this law, however it comes up often and should be noted, or practiced if it suits you. This concept states that whatever spell or magical act is being performed, the resulting energy created from that act will go into the Universe, and come back to the practioner three times.

You may or may not be familiar with this concept, and it has origins in other cultural practices, especially those of Eastern religions that believe in the law of karma. Wicca is what gives it the concept of three times, the number bearing importance to the reality of the power you are wielding.

It might not happen in the way that you think, for example if you wish harm on someone else, you may have three separate instances of bad fortune as a result, or it could feel like the impact of the return is 3 times greater than it normally would be, like expecting to get paid $100 and getting paid $300.

The Threefold Law is just another way to help you keep a balance with your practice and ensure that you harm none, and that includes harming yourself with the energy of three coming back to you.

Elements in All Things

In Wiccan belief, there are five elements: earth, air, fire, water, ether, or spirit. During rituals and ceremonies and especially in the casting or consecrating of a circle, the five elements are called into balance the energies of the ritual or spell. Not all Wiccans practice with five elements and just use the 4 main ones, conserving spirit as represented by the deity that they worship.

These elements are the fundamental building blocks of all things on Earth and in the Universe. They are responsible for the great eternal cycle of life through creation and destruction, the birth-death-rebirth cycle. These forces of nature that are sacred to Wiccans are always a part of practice because they are the literal life force that binds all matter and all spirit.

These elements have been studied throughout time and were part of philosophies dating back to the early Greeks, who were also worshippers of deities and religions of nature. These concepts are found across continents throughout many religions and beliefs including in Egypt and Babylonia, Hinduism and Buddhism, and many more.

The elements are definitely a tool that must be used in your Wiccan practice and as you get further along in your understanding of your spell work and rituals, you will find how important and powerful they can truly be.

Starting with the Core Beliefs and Philosophies

This book is a Starter Kit to help you get ready for how to practice the art of Wicca. It is a creative reality that requires understanding of all these basic, core elements and understandings. Before you get started with your spells and craft, you need to have a knowledge of the best way to practice and the ideas and concepts that sets Wicca apart from other Pagan religions and practices.

The core beliefs and philosophies in this chapter are just a simple guide to get you started and you can find even more about these concepts in your searching and education of this craft. Consider this information a tool in your tool box; it is the foundation of the house you are going to build with your starter kit so that you are ready and prepared for the work ahead.

Great things are around the corner for you when you honor the choice to practice this wonderful energetic truth. It has power beyond measure and it exists in all things and the creative tools that you use to get more connected to the work of Wicca is what will help you design the practice that is right for you on your journey.

The building blocks of your Starter Kit are only the beginning to a full expression of true Wiccan ritual and practice. In the next chapter, you will learn about the presence and celebrations of the Sabbats and Esbats and the rhythm and cycles they afford to the energy of your ongoing Wiccan rewards.

Sabbats / Sun Cycles

Sabbats are the holidays, sometimes referred to as the "solar holidays", or time of the Sun, and are marked by the changing seasons through the Solstices and Equinoxes. There are 8 total holidays that are traditionally celebrated and they are the 4 solstices and equinoxes, as well as, another 4 holidays spread out through the year between these other major passages. The additional 4 tend to fall halfway between an equinox and a solstice.

You might find in your practices that some Wiccans refer to these times as the Greater and Lesser Sabbats, since the solstices and equinoxes tend to be considered as times of much more intense energy, and therefore greater in celebration and importance.

In your practice, it only really matters that you offer some reflection and time to appreciating these moments in the ever-changing cycles of the Earth. You will find that there are a variety of ways to celebrate and you may find yourself coming up with your own unique spells and rituals with your Starter Kit to practice these festivities.

Samhain (Lesser)

This holiday is what witch's note as the New Year. It is All Hallows Eve, or Halloween and it is the time of year when the veil is thin between the Earth and the spirit planes. This time marks the end of the Summer and the opening of the cold, Winter ahead, when the Sun is not as bright and the days are not as long. It is the cycle of the dying Sun and the welcoming of the darkness.

Many Wiccans also see this time as a moment of personal death and rebirth, when you go within and reflect upon what is coming in the next cycle. It is when the harvests of hard personal work and labor can be stored and you are reminded of where you just were and where you need to prepare to go before your great rebirth in the Spring months.

Many people celebrate this time by dressing as ghosts or spirits to honor the dead. It is often a time that honors passed love ones and the rituals involved at this time can be a gateway to communication with the world of the spirits.

Yule (Greater)

Yule is also known as the Winter Solstice and has its pre-Christian name and celebrations from Pagan worship of divine in nature. This day marks the shift in the Sun's appearance in the sky. It is the longest night of the year before the days begin to get longer again and bring the hope of more light as the Spring approaches.

It is a significant time for bringing light into the home by candle light and many will decorate their homes with the boughs and branches of pine and evergreen trees, as well as holly and mistletoe.

The Yule log is a great tradition for this day and is a symbol of light to be burned all night long, that recounts the energy of that life force in nature, and welcomes it back into the shifting seasons. This is also a good time for celebrating the Goddesses as this is their time of year, while the Sun's light is waned and the dark nights are long.

This is a great reflection time and it opens the pathway to getting ready for lighter days ahead

Imbolc (Lesser)

A time of renewal, purity, fertility and growth, this sacred holiday is in the power of the Goddess Brigid, a maiden form of the Triple Goddess. Occurring in the very beginning of February, it is a subtle opening to spring and the awakening of the maiden. The last frosts are occurring and the white of snow and ice begins to melt.

It is a time of release, to lct go uf the old and prepare for the new to come around the corner. A time of renewal approaches.

Ostara (Greater)

This is the Spring Equinox and is the perfect balance of light and dark. It is considered the marriage, or union, between the god and the goddess, or the sun and the moon, to bring light back into the world and herald new growth. Ostara is the goddess who represents this time of year. Her name comes from the word Oestre which is Greek for egg, like a new egg of spring, ready to hatch and bring forth new life.

It is a time to celebrate renewal and welcome the balance of the male and female energies of Earth and spirit, as well as your own internal balances.

Beltane (Lesser)

Many people refer to this holiday as May Day as it usually falls on the first day of May and marks the midway point between the equinox of Spring and the solstice of Summer. It is a calling to the power of the gods of fertility and abundance as people celebrate the consummation of the marriage of the god and goddess to plant new life in the soils of the Earth womb.

The maypole is a symbol of this time and is danced around to mark the occasion and bonfires are a prominent part of the festivities, calling attention to the growing power of the masculine energy of the sun as it grows in strength and length of time in the sky.

It is a time of bounty, abundance and fertility with the waxing sunlight and the great goddess of fertility, ready to give birth to the growing seed within her womb.

Litha (Greater)

Litha is another name for Summer Solstice, which falls in the month of June. It marks the moment in the cycle of Earth when the sun is at its greatest strength, before he begins to turn toward his time of waning in preparation for Autumn. This holiday is also occasionally referred to as Mid-Summer Night's Eve and is the time when the fairies come out and join in the fun and celebration. It has been seen as a good time for divination because of the magic of fairies being close by.

Another time to celebrate the energy of the Sun and the fiery passion that lives in the hotter brighter months of the year. This is a time to gather energy and prepare for the impending harvest that will carry you into Autumn.

Lughnasadh (Lesser)

Sometimes also referred to as Lammas, Lughnasadh is the beginning of the harvest and mark then ending of the Sun's greatest time. The goddess of fertility is giving birth to everything that grew in the soil of her womb over the light months. It is the beginning of the time when you must set aside and store the bounty of this great birthing to prepare for the colder months ahead. It is the preparing time for when the Earth becomes cold and rests and the underworld opens.

This is a time of thankfulness and gratitude, appreciating the bounty of Mother Earth and reflecting upon the offering of the Sun's energy and light in all of the plants and foods that are harvested.

Mabon (Greater)

Mabon heralds the time of the Autumnal Equinox and is the second harvest, the final being Samhain. This is the time of transition into the final moments of fertility and abundance, when the leaves begin to shift in color and welcome a new kind of late to the day.

It is a time of storage, preparation, protection, security and groundedness and wakes up the new hours of dawn and night before the witch's new year to begin the cycle all over again.

This is a powerful time to give thanks to the ageing god and goddess of the spirit world as the move into their crone years and the Great Mother rests from her time of giving her offspring to the cycles and celebrations of all life. We welcome the age of night and the time of the cold season to let the mother crone rest and rejuvenate before she brings life back into the world again in the Spring.

Esbats / Moon Cycles

Every four weeks, the moon is pregnant with the light of the Goddess, to light up the night sky. These monthly moon cycles work in tandem with the Sabbats, marking the Sun's journey, and the goddess moon is the counterpart of the Sun's light to bring watery balance to that heat.

During the esbats, the focus is on the moon and on the energy of the triple goddess (Maiden-Mother-Crone), celebrating her divine light. Some people work in groups or covens, like with the celebrations and festivities around the time of the Sabbats, but any solitary practitioner can celebrate either Sabbat or Esbat on their own, and join in the knowing and knowledge that many Wiccans across the globe are gazing at the same orb of light as you are. It is a powerful magic to perform all at once and why it is so important to make space for this time.

The Triple Goddess and Esbats

Like with a Sabbat celebration, ritual, or spell, the type of practice varies from person to person, or coven to coven. One thing that always remains true is the celebration of the triple goddess in conjunction with the moon ceremonies.

The Triple Goddess is the very one who comes throughout the year. In Spring, she is Maiden, joining in union with the God of the Sun before she becomes Mother in the Summer months, growing and gestating the rich fruits of Earth. Finally, she becomes Crone in the Autumn/ Winter months, when her energies are now that of a wise old woman who prepares for her rebirth into maidenhood once again.

It may be that during the Sabbat cycles, you prefer to honor a specific form of the Triple Goddess. For example, in Spring ritual esbats, you may find ways to celebrate the Maiden goddesses under the full moon light, like Brigid or Ostara, or the crone goddesses, such as Hecate, under the moons of Autumn and Winter.

Full Moon Rituals

It is common practice to hold a ceremony, ritual or cast a spell with the magic and power of the full moon shining down upon you. Wiccans who work in covens will have their own, specific work to do and if you are a solitary practitioner you will work with your own energies to determine the needs of the moon you are working with. You may be casting magic for personal reasons, or you may be using the power of the moon to bring peace and prosperity to all people. However, you choose to work with the full moon, a ritual or incantation is a common practice during an esbat.

That said, some esbats may only be a practice of gratitude and thanks; a moment of reverence for the great divine. It really only matters based on what kind of practice you have. It is also not a requirement that you name a specific deity or goddess. Many Wiccans will simply impart the name of the Triple Goddess and use her whole energy as a symbol of all power and energy of the moon and the cycles of life.

New Moon Rituals

Let's not forget about the New Moon. Wiccans don't always worship the full moon and it is a practice to choose an alternative cycle, in this case, the new moon. Some see it as the perfect beginning, or opening, to honor the goddess and you may find that there are a lot of covens or solitary practitioners who prefer to work with the energy of the dark moon, bringing attention to a ritual or spell, and letting it grow with the waxing moon.

It really depends on what kind of a witch you are or want to be and so you have the power of choice when it comes to esbat practices and rituals. Another common practice is to have esbats for 4 moons a month, honoring not just the full and new moons, but also the first and last quarter moons.

Asking for all wisdom from the moon's waxing and waning is a powerful way to continuously honor the goddess and the cycles of the year. When in conjunction with the sabbats, or sun cycles, the esbats are a powerful source of connection to the divine rhythms of life in your Wicca work.

Wicca 101

This brief introduction to Wicca is just a starting point, an egg of Spring, to get you started with your practice. It is an important part of any magical starter kit to have the knowledge of what you are getting ready to align with and it is important that you grasp the traditions, philosophies and beliefs, before you get started with your practice.

You may find a great deal more information out there in the world, and you certainly should keep looking and asking questions. The world of Wicca is vast and broad, and speaks to a variety of different methods, deities, rituals and spells.

You will want to know more and more as you go and this Starter Kit is a great way to get you all pumped up with magical life force so that you can start practicing today. When you are ready to practice, you can use my other book, *Wicca for Beginners: A Basic Guide for the Modern Age to Learn About the Mysteries of Wiccan Beliefs and History, and How to Use Candles, Crystals, Herbs, Magik Rituals and Spells*, to help guide you through even more details of Wiccan worship, spells and rituals, to keep you on the right track with your study of this magical craft.

Chapter 2: What Do You Need? Basic Tools for Wicca

Wicca is a creative practice and there aren't any doctrines on how to practice it; there are guidelines, beliefs and philosophies asking you to perform magic in responsible ways. The tools that you choose to use are entirely up to you and you may take great pleasure in designing some of your own. It is an exciting journey to create your magic with your own, homemade tools, and once you are feeling more confident in your knowledge and practice, you will honor that side of your magic skills.

In the meantime, to get you started, this chapter demonstrates a list of some of the more commonly used tools to practice rituals and spells. You may not need, or want, all of these items to start, but it is a good foundation for understanding some of what you might be working with on your journey.

Acquiring Tools for the Starter Kit

There are many ways to build your tool box and you don't have to go out and spend a bunch of money to get what you need. There are always alternatives to the more expensive items you may find in a New-Age shop or online, but if you have a curiosity to find your items in this way, by all means. There is something good about holding something in your hand before buying it, and although online shopping is a convenience, it might not always be the best choice when acquiring your sacred tools, unless it is from a trusted source.

The fun of Wicca is how creative it is and that you can have a good time looking for objects from what you already own and may have, that will give you exactly what you need. It may be that you have some old kitchen items that could seem entirely non-magical, but once you give them a blessing and consecrate them to perform magic, they will look altogether different to you and will make excellent altar tools moving forward.

You can also make a lot of your own tools, if you're crafty and want to get really creative, or you can slowly collect things from local shops and also from nature. The most magical way to gain access to the tools you really want is to deliver your intention to the universe and ask for the right ones to come to you. Keep your eyes peeled as they will slowly begin to show up and maybe when you least expect it to happen. Sometimes, they might be a gift, and other times, you could trip over it in a parking lot outside the grocery store. You never know with magic, so keep an eye out for any tools you are attempting to draw to yourself.

Cleansing Your Tools

Before you use any tool that you acquire, it is important that you cleanse and consecrate your tools to rid them of any former energy and make them your own for magical purposes. Everything is energy and everything carries energy, and so even if you are ordering something from online that says it has already been cleansed or consecrated, cleanse it anyway.

Your magical tools need to carry a pure essence of you and your practice and a simple cleansing ritual is easy enough to perform with your number one tool, the elements and the casting of a circle. It's all about intentions and so you can use incense to smudge the energy while you incant some words about your purposes with the tools, offering that any former ownership and reality be released. It doesn't need to be complicated, just intentional.

Use Your Intuition to Gather Your Tools

It always depends on the ritual and what you are wanting to accomplish, but a general rule of thumb is that you have a tool to represent each element in your circle, i.e., earth, air, fire, water. You will see in further sections what represents which, but for now, you can get an idea that your ritual tools are here to help advise the energy of the spell work you are doing.

The most important thing is that you feel drawn to whatever tool you are using, and that you have an energetic connection to it. Depending on the ritual you are doing, if a certain tool doesn't feel quite right, don't use it. It may not be the right energy for your spell and that's okay. The practice of Wicca involves the practice of intuition and how to honor what *feels* right for each new experience of magic.

Tools are not a strict component of Wicca magic, and you may have senses at times not to use any tools and that all you need is yourself and nature and that is perfectly acceptable. You can use your own personal power and energy to draw upon the divine life forces, but this can take some time and practice, and so while getting started, having your altar of tools is a good way to honor and direct the energies you need to hold and work with.

Let's take a look at the tools you may want to bring into your practice and how they can influence your spells and rituals.

The Elements

Why the elements are considered a tool in Wicca? The 4 main elements, together with the fifth of spirit, are one of the tools you will use most often in your practice. Almost every time you are performing a ritual, you will honor and call the elements into your circle. If anything, the elements are the number one tool in your tool kit and should be considered as such.

Consider them a tool of connection to the divine and your magic for setting intentions of protection and manifestation. These elements are always present in any magic you work and are there to broaden your degrees of magical force by how you incorporate them into your spells.

The elements are usually invoked at the start of a ritual, each element being associated with a cardinal direction- North, East, South, West, or Earth, Air, Fire, Water. Typically, when using these tools, you will honor them by facing each direction that they represent. You may find it handy to have a compass with you, if you are uncertain of which direction is where. This act is sometimes referred to as "calling the quarters", which is just the act of calling the elements and the directions. Usually, the same action is performed at the closing of the ritual or circle in the same way that it was opened.

Furthermore, every element can be represented by several of the tools you will learn about in this chapter. An example of this might be that the pentacle symbol is a representation of the Earth element and the North and can be included in your rituals from earthly grounding and bringing focus to earth energies. Another example would be candle flame representing the element of fire and so on.

The same is true of every crystal and herb that you use in your practice. They all have individual qualities and properties to be studied and will always have a link to one of the elements, and sometimes more than one, depending on your own personal intuition about what you are working with. Objects carry the same impact. River stones represent water, but could also be considered earth, depending on your practice. Feathers can represent air, and so on.

The Elements are your number one tool so get comfortable and familiar with them and what they might represent in your tool box.

The Cauldron

This tool has been associated with witchcraft throughout history and popular culture. It is an icon of magic and has been shown as a major tool in the work of the witch. It is the cooking pot of magic and is associated with both fire and water. The cauldron holds the water, potion or brew, and yet it cannot boil and manifest without the heat and flame of the fire burning under its belly.

In the traditions of Wicca, it represents the creative force of transformation as represented by the Goddess. The Goddess exists in all her forms through the seasons of the year, just as the cauldron ignites the same transformation in anything it carries inside of it.

In modern times, the cauldron is not crucial to your practice, but it is a great tool for magical work, especially with fire or a place for safely burning candles and other magical elements, like herbs and incense. You may even want to use it to brew a potion, however you will need to have the ability to light a pretty roaring fire underneath it, which isn't really easy or ideal for indoor magical work.

Another effect of the cauldron is its use for scrying and divination. A bit of sacred water in the cauldron to gaze upon will open some pathways into the secrets of the divine. On the altar, it can be your pot for incense and the burning of magical herbs.

You can purchase cauldrons in shops and at an online magic store as well. They are not as easy to find as say, candles or incense, but they are a great addition to your starter kit. They come in a variety of sizes that you can choose from based on your needs. A smaller sized cauldron is best for a solitary practitioner, or any kind of indoor altar or work space. They come in a variety of metals, though cast-iron is the typical form and they rest on three legs with a handle for carrying it safely. If you cannot find a cauldron, that's ok! You can use another kind of heat-safe bowl that will be just as magical until you find the cauldron you have called upon to find you.

The Athame

Considered the element of fire (or air, depending on what Wiccan magic you are practicing) the athame is a blade or a sword that is used for direct and cutting energy, embodying transformation. It has a strong, masculine encrgy and would therefore be associated with god energy, rather than goddess. Swords are forged in fire and the metal of the blade, once melted and liquid, is channeled into becoming a sturdy blade of intention and purpose.

It looks like a dagger and traditionally has a black handle, or hilt and is typically no longer than your hand's length. They can be found in shops, or received as gifts, and are a lot harder to make on your own, compared to some of the other tools. You can sometimes even find athames in online or local shops whose blades are made of crystal or stone. If you cannot afford a fancy athame, you can actually just consecrate and small kitchen knife and adopt it into your magical tool box, giving it the authority and power of your Wiccan practice.

In general, the cutting of anything with an athame is purely symbolic in the ritual sense, however, in today's practices, modern Wiccans will use their athame to cut herbs in the wild, carve there wands and cut the branch or twig from the tree, and carve pentacles and other magical symbols into various spells and ritual materials.

Wicca will always want a fire element and a dagger, or athame, is a perfect blend of the fiery and masculine energy of the sun, along with its direct force to cut through energy and bring about a powerful fullness to your rituals. Keep an athame as a tool and be sure to cleanse it often with your other magical tools.

The Chalice

Chalice is a fancy word for cup, or goblet. It is connected to the element of water and the spirit of the Goddess. It symbolizes abundance and fertility, taking on many roles in the rituals and spells you choose to perform. It is often seen as an offering, or a way to give gifts, or libations to the deities called into your ceremony. Depending on your ritual, it can hold whatever liquid seems fitting: water, wine, ale, tea, kombucha, essences, potions. Conversely, an empty chalice can be symbolic in particular rituals, denoting an openness to receive abundance to be poured into the cup from the spiritual plane.

In most traditional Wiccan practice, the chalice is a silver color and made of metal as a representation of the Goddess and the moon. You might not want to drink from a silver plated or pewter cup, however, so even if you find one like this at a Magic Shoppe, you are likely not going to be able to regularly drink out of it because of toxic chemicals and elements. Certain beverages can actually corrode these metals and not be safe for ingestion.

It isn't a must have when you are building your tool kit and you can bless and consecrate any cup that you find that feels like the right choice for your altar and your particular choice of honoring the great divine. You may already have one that you know of that will be perfect for your uses and all you need to do is set magical intentions around it.

A wine glass can be just as effective as a goblet you buy at a neo-pagan shop. There could also be a cup that has been in your family for a long time that would be an excellent choice, honoring your ancestors with your magic chalice. You can also keep on the lookout for something to jump out at you when your shopping around town. It is always best to avoid plastic and synthetic materials in any of the tools you are acquiring for your magical purposes.

Whatever cup you choose, treat it differently than your other cups. It doesn't belong in the dishwasher and should be hand washed as it is used for magical purposes and should be considered sacred to you and your practice.

The Incense and Smoke

Incense has been a part of many religious cultures since the times of antiquity. It has always wafted through the halls and realms of focused intentional practices of connection to spirit and continues to be a large part of various cultural rituals today. It is an aromatic tool that brings together the earthly elements of herbs, spices, tree barks, oils and resins, to them manifest a smoke of cleansing purity, creating sacred space and air in the atmosphere. It is associated with the element of Air (and sometimes fire) and is a regularly utilized component of Wiccan ritual and spell.

Traditional methods for burning incense include the use of loose herbs in some kind of censer. A censer is a hanging container that can be swung from a rope, a chain or a handle. You will often see Catholic priests using a censer in their rituals. You can also use your small cauldron to work as a censer and waft the smoke around like that, allowing it to continue to burn in your cauldron while you perform your rituals.

Loose incense can be tricky to work with. You need more than just the herbs and will usually need some charcoal bricks or disks, sold alongside incense in many shops. These days, a more popular form of incense is sticks or cones, which can be easier and sometimes safer to burn, depending on your set up and your chosen tools and methods. Either method you choose will work wonderfully.

You can also find what are known as smudge sticks which are typically just a bundle of wrapped, dried herbs that you can light and then let smoke. Smudging is another popular form of working with air energy to consecrate your sacred space. Palo Santo is a sacred, harvested wood, that can be lit and burned for the same purposes and comes in small sticks.

Burning incense is often considered an offering to whatever deities you are connecting with and you can burn incense to an image of them on your altar, or set the intention that you are focused on that particular god or goddess as it burns. Using incense during your rituals and spells is very powerful and you may alter which scent you are using based on your spell. The earthly materials used to make incense, such as herbs and spices, all carry specific energies, so you will want to make sure you are working with the right aromatic energy for your spell work.

Smoke is purifying and cleansing and great for removing unwanted energies. It has an ability to prepare for Wiccan work and also to cast a circle. It is a powerful tool that should be used frequently in all of your magical endeavors.

The Candle

The candle is a symbol of all of the elements. The wick is the Earth and must be present to ground the candle and keep is alight and burning. The wax is water in that it melts and turns to a liquid state and also evaporates, demonstrating the transformative qualities of water. Air is required to keep the candle flame burning, as without oxygen, there could be no fire. The flame is obvious: fire. When you charge the candle with intentions of bringing spirit into the elements of the candle, you are adding the fifth element. All five elements together in one candle equals a powerful tool of magic, uniting all of the forces of the universe together in one little tool.

Candles allow us to bring the magical power of color into our spell work and craft. Certain colors are associated with certain qualities and characteristics of life and can be useful representation in magical practice. Corresponding colors to corresponding spells, make for an even more powerful intention and manifestation.

You can create even more abundant power in your candle tool by anointing it with sacred or magical oils and scents to carry your message even farther. Working with certain herbs and consecrated oils will always give the energy of your candle magic more power and so with the combination of all of the elements, the possibilities of color magic and the enhancement of power through oils and herbs, the candle is a very powerful little tool that should be incorporated in to almost every ritual.

The Crystal and the Stone

Crystal can be a broad term to describe a number of solid objects used in the practice of Wicca. Crystals are simply put, minerals. Minerals are considered inorganic substances that form naturally and grown naturally underground in the Earth. Why they would be called "inorganic" by science is beyond the heart and mind of a Wiccan, who embraces minerals and crystals as living things. Each unique crystal, stone and mineral has its own unique energy and chemical composition and therefore each represents very different energies and qualities.

The molecular structure of most minerals is what causes their unique shapes and patterns, and creates some flat surfaces and interesting geometric structures. Common crystals that are used frequently in magical practices are quartz crystal, rose quartz, amethyst and more. These are crystalline unlike some of the other items known as gems stones that are equally valuable in the use of magic. Some examples of these stones are jade, kyanite, lapis lazuli, tiger's eye and so forth. These stones are combinations of several minerals, unlike their crystalline friends, and so are not what we call 'true crystals', but they still have very potent energy and power.

Crystals and stones, no matter how you call them, are gifts from the Earth and contain powerful magic. They are regularly used tools in magic circles and Wiccan practices. They can be used for healing the energy of the self, as well as plants and animals. You can even plant crystals in your garden for a healing power in your soil and to help your seeds and plant growth flourish. Crystals and stones have an electric charge and are sensitive to the elements. They are conduits of energy and can help bring in and send out energy through your ritual practices. Keeping a family of crystals and stones to use in your Wicca practice is a simple way to bring more manifestation and power to your everyday rituals and spells.

They can be used to mark your sacred circle when you are casting your opening rituals. They can be used to honor specific deities that are related to specific stones. They can alter and shift your energy from a low to a high vibration when used in personal energy clearing. They can be worn as jewelry for protection. They can be used in charms, amulets and sachets. You can use them for scrying and divination, or simply to add more focus to your ritual.

Consider also the use of color magic with crystals and stones. They come in a wide range of magical colors and so depending on your work, the added advantage of specific stones and the colors that they bring can further enhance your methods of manifestation.

The Herbs

Herbs are most definitely tools when it comes to Wicca. The lore and history behind herbal magic is incredibly extensive, and is one of the main components of any kind of healing herbal remedy or magic spell used in various forms of Paganism.

Herbs have a special past with the witches of old and have been around longer than any other drug or remedy, and will continue to out live and outlast the drugstore medications that are so common today.

Aside from their healing benefits, which should definitely be explored by any solitary Wiccan, they all have very powerful magical properties. You will find that an assortment of herbs grown in your backyard garden will always come in handy for your rituals and craft work.

People will use herbs to decorate their altars for Sabbats and Esbats and will also carry them around on their person for protection or other magical means. The use of herbs as a tool in Wicca is something to get used to and acquainted with. They are versatile and will serve a variety of purposes with all of the spells you work.

Keeping a cupboard of dried herbs is a beneficial thing to do, if you are regularly practicing Wicca and you will need to consider them just as important as any other tool on the list. You may use them to burn as incense, to make a charm or sachet, or even for a spell that is meant as a healing remedy ritual, taking your herbs in the form of a tea, tincture or broth.

All of your herbs can be charged and consecrated before use, just like any of your other tools. As you practice more of your Wicca rituals and spells, you will find more and more creative uses for the wide variety of herbs available and what all of their magical purposes are.

The Pentacle

Not every pentacle is a five-pointed star, however that is the most commonly inscribed symbol that is often termed as the pentacle.

A pentacle is simply a disk-like slab that can have one or multiple magical symbols inscribed on it. In Wicca, the most common is the five-pointed star, and so for the purposes of this book, you can assume that when I refer to a pentacle, that is the shape I am referring to. The five-pointed star is also called a pentagram, which makes it an easy word to associate with a common pentacle. Pentagram to pentacle.

The pentagram is an ancient sign and symbol that has been found all over the world in various cultures to represent a variety of aspects of the human mind, body and spirit. It is an Earth symbol and when you look at the sacred Tarot deck, the earthly symbols on the cards are represented by the pentacle pentagram. The points of the star represent the elements, the point at the top being spirit. The rounded shape and earth quality associate it strongly with the Goddess.

Wiccans will inscribe a pentacle on many of their magical tools, like in the hilt of their athame, or on the cover of their Book of Shadows. It can also be used as a symbol drawn in the air and with a wand or blade, and even with a smoking incense or smudge stick, to consecrate the area or the ritual. It is a helpful symbol of protection from harmful or possibly negative energies, as well as a powerful tool of manifestation.

If you have a large pentacle, you may even like to use it as a consecration tool by setting your other magical tools or elements, like candles or crystals, on top of the pentacle to imbue it with that sacred, symbolic energy. You can even carve a pentacle into the wax of a candle for ritual and spell work purposes, or simply draw it on objects with marker or ink.

You can find pentacles at a majority of magical shops and online retailers. They come in a variety of shapes and sizes and also materials. Many wiccans will wear a pentacle as a talisman or amulet of protection and as a symbol of their craft.

You may be a creative person and will want to make your own pentacle from your own materials at home. There really isn't a right or a wrong way to do it, as long as you are using your manifestation of magic to create it for your ritual purposes. Use paper and pen if you have nothing else, but you can sculpt it out of clay, carve it into wood, paint it on a canvas; the possibilities are endless.

The pentacle is a magical tool for your starter kit that brings a powerful elemental symbol of protection and manifestation. Use it wisely and freely.

The Wand

The wand is a popular symbol of witchcraft and dates back to the ancestors of Egypt as well as that of the ancient Pagan cultures. Wands are symbols and tools of manifestation and direction and connect with the element of Air. In the Tarot, the air element is also represented by the suit of wands and deals with the power of thought and intentions.

Despite the popularity of certain magical witches and wizards in film and television in today's entertainment world, it is not the wand itself that contains the power; it is the witch who imbues the wand with their personal power and life force energy to transform and manifest through ritual intention. It is used to help direst energy in a subtle and gentle way (unlike the athame which is a bit more intense in its direction).

A wand is regularly used in rituals for invocations of the deities you are calling into your magic circle and can also be used for the drawing of magical symbols in the air, such as the pentagram, or pentacle symbols. This tool is more representative of the gods rather than goddesses, obvious in its phallic shape (also like the athame) but also because of how it directs energy with a more masculine force. Depending what kind of Wicca you practice, the wand, generally associated with air, can also be associated with fire because of its transformative abilities and magical properties. For the solitary Wiccan, you can choose whatever feels right for you, and in some covens, there may be a more deliberate or specific choice, based on that group.

Finding the right wand for you is an exciting journey and you can acquire them in a variety of ways. Many Wiccans will find their wands from the local magic shop and they have a wide range of styles, including some that are fashioned from crystals and gem stones, which harbor a lot of powerful energy.

Other wands can be made by your own hand, and for a creative witch, this is the best bet. Whatever wand you make with your own energy and power is going to create and even deeper magic for you. You can acquire the tools for your handmade wand from nature and will need to use your intuition to guide you to the right materials. You may find the perfect tree branch to turn into a wand, but you will always need to ask for permission from the tree first. Wait for the response and tell it what your intentions are with it. It may be excited to become your wand!

There are plenty of other natural gifts from the land that can be included in your wand-making endeavors: twigs, moss, feathers, leaves, anything that feels right for you. Whether you make a wand or you buy one it is a very helpful tool to give you more directness in your spells and rituals and helps you to bring more masculine energy and air element into your work.

The Book of Shadows

This is often one of the most treasured tools in a witch's arsenal of magic. Your Book of Shadows is your private and personal spell book that guides you in everything that you do. It is where all of your spells, rituals, symbols, prayers, poems, recipes and sacred information is kept. It is a great place for you to keep a record of your journey through Wicca as well, and it will change and evolve with your practice, like a powerful living energy.

In a coven it is their handbook that they adhere to as a group, and much of the information is passed down, like family traditions and stories. For a solitary practitioner, it is the best way for you to grow your practice and spells, one page at a time throughout the years. The history behind the Book of Shadows is long and it was Gerald Gardner who first coined the term for the wiccan practice. A Book of Shadows shared by others is often added to generationally and some Wiccans have even published their own version of the Book to help Wiccans setting off on their journey who need a good place to start.

You can build your own Book by utilizing the spells and rituals of those who came before you and add to it as you grow and evolve with your craft, manipulating and changing various spells to better suit your needs. It is a good way for you to organize the best and most useful spells that you find on your path. You may have a variety of books about the craft, but you only use an assortment of the various practices from your library of witchcraft. A Book of shadows is a nice way for you to collect the right information for your solitary practice and build your own spells out of it.

It is basically your Physician's Desk Reference for magic, and the more you add to it and use it, the better you will become at empowering your magical practice. You can decorate it however you like and find a particular notebook that resonates strongly with you and your energy. In these modern times, you can also keep your book of shadows in digital form, on your home computer, or even online on a website, to show others who are interested in your personal work. This can be good, however the use of physical formats, like ink and paper, has a more visceral impact in the work of spells and magic. You may want to consider transcribing your Book of Shadows digitally for safe keeping, but have an original copy that is a physical book.

This tool will be with you the whole way. It is your guide book and travel map through your rituals, spells and incantations and it will always be a grounding and supportive energy in your tool box.

The Tarot

The Tarot is a deck of 78 cards that each represent important archctypes and symbols. The origins of the Tarot are separate from Wiccan and other Pagan practices and have been around as early as the 1400's. People who are not at all interested in Wicca or magic find themselves drawn to this humble deck of cards. They are a way to answer questions through imagery and symbols and have been used in various forms of divination, prediction and manifestation.

The messages of the cards and the spread that they are in allow us to ask for a direct consultation with the divine life forces to gain knowledge and understanding of what is happening in our lives. It is a reflection of life, or a cosmic mirror, that allows the questioner to get a deeper truth to their queries. You can see beyond what you would normally choose to see and there are new angles to consider and support your path ahead.

The art of reading the Tarot cards is a whole other kind of magic that takes time and practice and when you bond with the cards, they bond with you, too. Many witches are very careful about how they come by their decks, or "choose" them. Some say they should only be given as a gift, and others note that it is best to be guided to the right deck to support your own power and magical purposes and intentions.

The standard deck is 78 cards, divided into a Major and Minor Arcana. Each section, and each card within that section, reflect inner truths and deeper, hidden knowledge. The whole deck is a long story of a traveler going through a journey and that journey is depicted in various images that support the natural powers of the Earth, including all five elements, as well as sun and moon energy, masculine and feminine polarities, and astrology.

The major Arcana are the most powerful cards in the deck and are indications that you will be experiencing powerful shifts and upheavals, whether good or bad, in your life. The characters on the cards, or archetypes, represent an important stage in the questioner's journey ranging from the pure innocence of the Fool, to the hard-earned wisdom of the World. There are deep and meaningful lessons shown in the Major Arcana and it is a good choice to pay attention when these cards show up as an influence.

The rest of the deck is the Minor Arcana and is very similar to a deck of regular playing cards. Each number, from Ace to 10, has each element associated with it on a different card. There are 4 aces in the deck, one for Earth, Air, Fire and Water. Therefore, it is for the Two, the three and so on. They are depicted on the cards, instead of as the elements, as the Pentacles, Wands,

Swords, and Cups. Look familiar? All of the suits are represented by the tools you are learning about to represent your magical work with your practice.

These cards are thought to be more in relationship to the every day actions we take in life, rather than the profound spiritual journey of the Major Arcana. They cover the elements of the experience, not the experience itself. Those elements fall into the categories of manifestation and groundedness (pentacles), ideas and thoughts (wands), action and direction (swords), and feelings and emotions (cups).

As you can see, there is overlap and connection between the Tarot and Wicca, as well as other forms of witchcraft. The cards are even linked to other occult philosophies including numerology and astrology. Each card can be linked to a celestial body or zodiac sign, as well as a number, based on the card's suit and where it falls in the order for the deck.

Tarot can be incorporated as symbolic representations of certain elements or factors in your spell work and rituals. You can use each card for specific reasons, like a Full Moon ritual incorporating The Moon card on your altar or in your spells, or the use of the Sun card in a prosperity or abundance spell. You can even use the deck as a consult to help you design your spells and rituals.

Tarot cards are universally used for a variety of reasons and have very close ties to the practice of Wicca. They are an incredible tool to help with divination and consulting the divine to help you manifest the right part of your journey through your rituals and spells.

Your Tool Box and Starter Kit

Each of the tools listed in this chapter are a great starting point for any Wiccan. Each one may come to you as a separate influence at different times, as you build upon your tool box, or you may find them all at once and can begin right away with cleansing and consecrating them for your magical purposes.

Be clear with what you want your tools to be. Build your altar and your tool kit with your own creative abundance and energy. If you are interested in being in a coven, you may be guided by your group to acquire specific tools. For the solitary practitioner, you can govern your own choices a little more freely and take your time in finding what tools feel right for you.

Use your intuition and ask for what you want. Let the tools find you and be ready for them when they do. In the next step, you will learn about what it takes to create an altar using all of your magical tools to get you started.

Chapter 3: Step by Step Guide to Altars

What is an altar? Altars have existed throughout cultures, religions and across time, and to this day continue to represent a physical embodiment of our worship for the divine. It is the place where we honor our gods, goddesses, ancestors and spirits and is the great focus point of any ritual, celebration, spell, meditation and prayer. The altar of your making is the centerpiece of your wiccan practice and it continuously holds space for all of the elements of the divine that you bring into your life.

Wiccan altars can be built inside or out, or both. Since you aren't performing rituals all day long, they are often located in places where they can be off to the side, but seen regularly, or pulled out to be presented in the center of the room for spell work and rituals. Typically, all of the tools that you use for your craftwork and spells remain on the altar at all times and can usually be seen as part of the altar. If you have an outdoor altar, you may use a completely different set of tools than you would for your indoor altar.

As you read in the last chapter, the tools that you use are symbols for the divine aspects of nature that Wicca recognizes and asserts as part of the magic of connection with the rhythms and cycles of all life. This includes the tool of the five elements and the gods and goddesses that are chosen for worship. Some altars reflect the appreciation of these deities through the display of images or figurines to honor that specific deity, as well as the elements represented by candles, chalice, athame, wand, and other tools.

Many altars strive to incorporate the elements by adding a dish of water as well as a bowl of salt (salt can be replaced with soil or sand to represent earth energy). The candle is the fire and an altar incense holder or burner is usually present to represent air. Another tool that was not listed in the last chapter, but has been often used in ritual practice and to decorate an altar is a bell.

A bell is a great way to call attention to your altar and let that sound wave energy ring out that you are honoring the altar of magic. Bell tones are also very opening and help you focus your energy and the energy all around into devotion. An altar bell is a great source of calling power to what the altar represents to you.

How to Build an Altar: Step by Step Instructions

Here is where to begin when building your altar. Take it one step at a time and remember that your altar will evolve with your practice and so it doesn't need to be perfect from the beginning. Work with what you've got and go from there.

Step 1: Pick the Best Spot

Your altar could take any number of forms and be housed in a variety of locations. You might have a built-in shelf or cabinet in your home that is the perfect size and location, or you may need to use a piece of furniture that will act as a flat surface where you can set your altar up.

You may not be able to afford to run out and buy a new piece of furniture to act as your altar and so a temporary solution, like a desk or a coffee table, will work just as well. You can place it somewhere where it won't be in the way and pull it out as needed for your rituals and spell work.

Many people will use a square or rectangular surface, but many Wiccans enjoy a round table top as it is easiest to maneuver around and has a close connection to the moon, the sun and the goddess as well as other symbols in the craft.

Typically, altars are made of natural materials and it is best to try and choose furniture or places to put your altar that are made of wood, or occasionally metal. A glass surface is also common. Generally, it is common to use a cloth or a tapestry of some kind to cover the surface of the table it is on. This cloth can be magically charged through a ritual.

Wherever you choose to set up your altar it needs to have the following elements:

- Accessible

- Made of natural elements (if possible)

- Movable (if possible or desired)

- Visible to you at all times (if preferred- you may also choose to keep it hidden in a cupboard or covered with a cloth to prevent visitors from tampering with it)

Once you have the space and the surface that you want your altar to be in, you can begin to set it up and prepare it for ritual magic and spell work.

Step 2: Setting up your Altar

1. Cover the surface with your preferred cloth. It can have been charged with protective energy, or you may have a meaningful garment, like a scarf, from a passed relative or ancestor. Whatever your cloth is, it is meant to set the tone for your altar space and it may get dirty with candle wax, ashes, or other herbs, incense and magical tools, so make sure it is a cloth you don't mind getting smudge with magical use.

2. Determine a center piece for your altar and display it. The central focus of it could be a particular image of a god or goddess, a pentacle, a candle, a large geode, crystal or stone. It is up to you to decide how you want to create focus for your altar and bring your attention to the center of your magical practice. Starting with the center focus point is good, because you can build around it with your other tools.

3. Incorporate your tools, whatever they may be. You may want to determine at this point what direction your altar is facing. This could also play a part in where you choose to place your altar. You may prefer that it faces a certain direction and so you will need to accommodate that first, before setting up the rest of it. When you are laying out your sacred tools, you may want to arrange them in their corresponding cardinal directions. For example:

- Place the athame (fire) to the south position

- Place the chalice (water) in the west position

- Place the incense (air) in the east position

- Place the pentacle (earth) in the north position

Placing your tools in the directions they represent will help you keep a focus on the elements and their performance in your rituals. You can also fill the chalice with water, add a bowl of soil or salt, instead of using a pentacle, feather for the eastern air and your candles in the place of the south. It is up to you what items you decide to place, but they should all be a regular part of your magical rituals.

4. Another placement option is to put your Goddess tools on the left (Earth and Water) and the tools representative of the God on the right (Fire and Air). It truly depends on what kind of Wicca you want to celebrate on your altar.

5. Eclectic practitioners (usually solitary) will build and construct their altar based on personal ideas and choices and so it can follow any natural pattern and layout based on your own 'eclectic' practice.

6. Consecrate your altar by lighting your candle and incense and calling upon the elements to bless your space. You can cast a circle, or perform a ritual (see Chapters 4 and 5) at this point, or you can keep it simple and just bring focus and intention to celebrating the creation of your altar with a few simple tools and words. Let your candle burn until it goes out and keep some incense lit, just to bring the altar to life.

7. Keep your altar clean, organized, and respected. You may need to do regular cleansing and purifying of your ritual tools as you use your altar more and more. Keep the altar fresh and fluid so that your magic doesn't become stagnate.

8. Decorate your altar according to whatever holiday you are celebrating. Your entire home may become like an altar at

Yule time or Samhain, but your physical altar needs some extra special ingredients to help you honor the Wheel of the Year and to stay tidy throughout all the seasons.

Step 3: Clearing and Charging Your Altar and Tools

Your tools and your altar can collect unwanted or negative energy over time. Even brand-new tools that you get from the internet can contain unwanted energy that needs clearing, coming from the manufacturing, packaging and shipping processes. During spells and rituals, or even having a lot of guests in your home around your altar, your space and the tools that you use can acquire and absorb energy that needs clearing.

It is a good regular practice to get into and is quite easy to do. Depending on what object you are working to clear, you may need a different purifying agent. Let's take a look at what some of them are:

1. *Salt*

   Salt is a very powerful cleansing agent for denser energies and it may be used on your crystals and stones and even some candles and other tools. You may want to make sure that the salt won't damage the item you are trying to cleanse through a chemical reaction. Research may be necessary.

   - Bury your stones and crystals in a dish or bowl of sea salt over night

- Bathe your tools in warm salt water (precautions may be necessary- salt reactions can damage metals)

- Sprinkle salt on your altar

2. *Sunshine/ Moonshine*

The power of light can create a good deal of cleansing energy. The Sun light is strong and intense and the warmth and heat of the sun is good for any tool. You can simply set your tools in a safe place out doors throughout the day in order to burn out any unwanted, or collected energies.

The same can be done with Moonlight and it just depends on what you are going for. A full moon is the best time for cleansing your tools, so you may need to time your purification according to an Esbat. You could also use the full sun of the day and carry your cleansing through the night of the full moon, bringing your tools back into your altar at dawn, giving them both the Sun and the Moon's energy of purification (both masculine and feminine/ god and goddess energy)

3. *Soil*

Soil is incredibly grounding and can transmute any energy it touches. It is the very Earth that pulls all of our energy and so you can use it to clear and ground yourself, so why not your tools.

To use soil as a clearing and purifying agent, you can simply bury your tools underground overnight. If are worried about your tools getting dirty, wrap them in cloth first, and then lay them in the soil, covering them all the way with the dirt. Dig them out in the morning and return them to your altar with a blessing.

4. *Incense/ Smudging*

Incense, or smudge sticks are a perfect way to cleanse your tools when the above three options aren't advisable, or convenient. Smoke clears away a lot of energy, especially when you are using herbs specifically for cleansing. White Sage is a popular choice and there are other herbs you can use as well, such as rosemary and lavender.

All you have to do is let the smoke cover your tools. You can waft the smudge stick or incense over it, or you can wave your tool through the smoke. It is also a great way to cleanse and refresh the energy of the whole entire altar, which isn't really easy to bury in salt or soil, or carry outside into the sun and moonlight.

Step 4: Charging Your Altar Tools and Implements

Once you have cleansed the energy of the altar and your tools, you can now charge them with the energy you need to, such as whatever your intention for a spell might be. You might also simply want to charge the energy of the altar and the tools to help them rest well between rituals and spell work, after they have been cleansed and before returning them to their places on the altar.

You can charge just about any tool with your intentions. Intention is the key and the key to setting an intention within your tools is focus. Here are some guidelines to charging your instruments after you have purified them:

Step 1: Simply Hold it In Your Hand and Send the Energy of Intention In

This may not sound very magical, but oh, how it is! We are pure energy and part of Wicca is understanding that concept. When you hold something in your hand, let's say it is a quartz crystal, and you are wanting to charge it with the energy of clarity and focused divination, you are telling the energy of that crystal in your hand, with your own energy, what you want it to carry. That stone will then be available to you with that energy anytime you call upon it.

You can do the same thing with a candle that you are going to use in a spell, charging it in your hand with your powerful intentions by asking it to receive the energy of what you are trying to manifest. When you light the candle, you are lighting the energy of your intentions.

Step 2: Sunlight and Moonlight, Again

You have already seen that both sunlight and moonlight can cleanse and purify your tools. Well, they can also charge them with their powerful energy. You can kill two birds with one stone, as the saying goes, by using the energy of the sun/ moon to both cleanse and charge whatever tools you are working with.

The important factor is that you set very clear intentions with how you want your tools to be charged. Writing your intention down on paper and then laying the tools on top of that paper in the sun/moon light, is one powerful option. You can also talk it out aloud as you are laying the tools out, suggesting that as the energy clears from the tools, that they be filled with [insert intention or magical purpose here].

You get the drift. The sun and the moon work both ways, as long as you are clear about your intentions for manifestation.

Step 3: Using Other Tools to Charge Your Tools

Depending on what your ritual or spell is, you may end up using a variety of tools from your altar to charge the energy of another. You may not need all of them charged in the same way and so you can use any number of your available tools to increase strength and focus on your intention setting and charging ritual.

One example might be using a pentacle slab out in the sunshine and placing whatever tool you want to charge on top of the pentacle. Set your intention and let the pentacle's already existing power imbue your tools with more energy. Another example might be pointing your wand or athame at the tool to be charged while you intone or incant some words of power into it.

This can be a very direct and focused way to help you charge your tools. The use of other tools will always bring more energy and power to something, as long as the intention you are desiring is behind it.

Step 4: Visualization is Key

Use your third eye to set intentions and charge your tools and your altar. Wicca celebrates your connection to your own psychic sense and your ability to connect to your higher knowing and higher sight. When you are working with your tools and altar, you can use creative visualization in the mind's eye to help charge your tools.

Picture what you want your tools to have within them energetically. See an image in your head of what that might look like. For example, say you are trying to charge a stone or crystal with healing energy. Close your eyes and see a color for healing, whatever that color is for you (gold, green, and turquoise are common). See a bright light in that color radiating out of the stone, as you speak words to charge that energy, or simply by holding it in your hand while you picture colorful light radiating out of it.

Visualization, coupled with some other charging steps can make a huge difference in the energy you put into your magical objects.

Step 5: Use Your Words

Words are important and the words that you use are a major part of your entire practice and how you manifest magic. When you are charging your tools, it doesn't have to be fancy. It can be as simple as this:

I charge this [name the tool or object]

through the power of the divine

to bring [name the magical intention]

into my life.

Therefore, it is!

If you want to get a little fancier, by all means. The more specific you are, the better, and so much of the spell casting and ritual words that are used in Wicca are like little poems and songs. Don't be afraid to rhyme and have fun:

By the light of this moon, on this third day of June,

I open this object to light.

I say a big prayer, to offer through air,

The message of clearing my sight.

Let this crystal appear, whenever I am near,

And show me more of my dreams.

A diviner's stone, I let it be shone,

By the moon, So mote it be!

Step 6: Consecrating Your Tools for Your Altar

Consecration of your tools usually goes hand in hand with your charging of them, but you don't have to do this, if you are not ready to invoke deities or external energies from outside of yourself. Typically, consecration is a bit more elaborate and may involve more, or all of your tools. You will want to invoke your deity of choice for this and will also likely want to cast a circle for the experience.

It may seem like a lot of effort, but when you experience the energy that results from this powerful cleansing, charging and consecration, you will understand right away. Try doing a spell without cleansing, charging and/or consecrating your tools and then try it again after you do. Notice the difference, and you will notice just how powerful these energies truly are.

In the next chapter, you will get more acquainted with your Wicca Starter Kit's guide to casting a circle. Now that you have your tools and your altar all set up, the next big step is casting the energy circle and calling in the elements and the deities. It is the basics of spell casting and ritual in Wicca.

Chapter 4: Step by Step Guide to Casting A Circle

Casting a circle in Wicca is the butter you put on your bread. It is the opening moment to connect you to your ritual, spell, or prayer, and creates a focused intention of protection while you work with the divine energies. Yo can create your own version of circle casting based on what you read here, but as a Starter Kit Guide, this chapter will show you the step-by-step path to opening a simple circle for quick and easy endeavors, and a more elaborate, ritual circle that will draw on my power and take a little more time and effort.

The basic circle, or the ritual circle both share the same components. The most important aspect is the honoring and calling in of the four directions. As you have ready throughout this book, the Elements are a tool for magic and each one of them corresponds to a cardinal direction. When you call upon the directions, you are also calling upon the Elements and can begin a more focused magical practice with these energies open to you.

Another key factor to remember is that your circle is meant to be a shield of protection from unwanted energies. When you open yourself to the divine, you can open yourself to a variety of other energies, and so your circle of magic is your protective shield to keep you safe during your rituals.

While you work with magic, you may choose to do more elaborate circle casting in the beginning and then use more simple forms of it later as you become more confident in your powers.

Take a look at these simple, step-by step guidelines to casting circles. Bring in your desired tools and your altar for added power.

Basic Circle Casting

Step 1: Where Will It Be?

Choosing where you are going to cast your circle depends on what your purposes are. You may be doing some kitchen magic with your cooking and your circle would only need to be the area where you are preparing your magical food.

You may also only need the space in front of your altar in order to say a blessing or a prayer, and that's it. For a simple and basic casting, all you have to decide is where you are going to be performing your craft and how much space you might need. If you are standing in one place the whole time, you won't need a very big circle.

Consider where you are going to cast it, before you cast.

Step 2: What Do I Need?

For a simple circle, you really only need yourself to cast. It can be as simple as pointing your finger towards the floor and finding north, going around in a clockwise direction and speaking to each direction.

You don't have to have all of your tools and candles and incense. You can just set the intentions with the power of your own energy and just use your hands, fingers, and eyes to point out the directions.

You may need a compass in general to help you point yourself in the right direction as you move around the circle.

Step 3: How to Open

When you cast your circle, use your creative visualization skills to actually picture a protective shield around you. It can look like a glass orb, or just a blanket of white light; whatever feels best for you.

1. Starting at the north position, point your finger, either on the floor, or directly in front of you as say, "I call upon the powers of the North and the element of Earth to guard and protect me as I open to the divine powers of all that be."

2. Move in a clockwise direction and find the East saying the following words: "I call upon the powers of the East and the element of Air to guard and protect me as I open to the divine powers of all that be."

3. Move in a clockwise direction and find the South saying the following words: "I call upon the powers of the South

and the element of Fire to guard and protect me as I open to the divine powers of all that be."

4. Move in a clockwise direction and find the West saying the following words: "I call upon the powers of the West and the element of Water to guard and protect me as I open to the divine powers of all that be."

5. Coming back to your starting point, you can put your palms together in a prayer pose, or hold your palms out to receive energy form the divine while you call upon the fifth element, Spirit, with the following words: "I call upon the energy of the Great Mother and the Universe to aid me in my magic. And so it is."

6. You can change the words in any way you prefer, or simply sense and think the idea of these words. You don't have to say them out loud in order to cast. It's all about intention.

7. Practice your intended magic!

Step 4: How to Close

1. Starting at the West position, where you ended the opening of your circle, point your finger, either on the floor, or directly in front of you as say, "I thank the powers

of the West and the element of Water for your guardianship and protection. And so it is."

2. Move in a counterclockwise direction and find the South saying the following words: "I thank the powers of the South and the element of Fire for your guardianship and protection. And so it is."

3. Move in a counter clockwise direction and find the East saying the following words: "I thank the powers of the East and the element of Air for your guardianship and protection. And so it is."

4. Move in a counter clockwise direction and find the North saying the following words: "I thank the powers of the North and the element of Earth for your guardianship and protection. And so it is."

5. Coming back to your starting point, you can put your palms together in a prayer pose, or hold your palms out to receive energy form the divine while you call upon the fifth element, Spirit, with the following words: "I give thanks to the divine for aiding me in my magical purpose. And so it is!"

Closing your circle is like opening it, except you start with the West and move counterclockwise back to the North, finalizing it with gratitude for whatever deities of spiritual life force you call upon to help you in your magical needs.

Ritual Circle Casting

For a more elaborate experience involving rituals, casting large spells, or celebrating Sabbats and Esbats, a ritual circle is a more detailed approach and considered more opening of powerful energy as well as more tools and set up.

It is a lot of fun to make a greater occasion out of the magic you are wanting to perform and so having access to all of your tools and making a bigger casting experience will help you connect more deeply to your divine power and the powers of spirit.

You won't need much in the way of decorations or elaborate planning. You will only need your altar and your tools that you have set up. There are several ways to go about this process and, like with any other kind of Wiccan magic, your creativity is always permitted and honored, so have fun modifying and inventing your own practices for casting.

Step 1: Where Will It Be?

As with your Basic Circle Casting, choosing the space appropriate to your needs is the first step. For a more elaborate circle, you may need to perform a lot more movement and preparation within your circle, so it may need to be big enough for you to dance around, or move to quite a few places.

If you are outdoors, you will need to determine the perimeter of where you need to cast. For an outdoor celebration, like a Sabbat or an Esbat, these types of circles may need more tools and preparations.

For ritual work, you will often want your altar to be a part of your circle and so finding a way to cast with your altar in the center or at a point of importance in your circle can be ideal, depending on what magical purposes you have.

Step 2: What Do I Need?

For a ritual circle casting you will want to incorporate more of your tools, including, but not limited

to the following:

- Earth element, like a bowl of salt, or soil; pentacle
- Air element, like incense and feathers, or any other object that might represent Air
- Fire element, like candles and athame
- Water element, like a chalice or bowl filled with water
- Wand
- Crystals and stones for your circle (optional)
- Matches/ lighter
- Compass (optional)
- Salt (optional)
- Chair, or pillow to sit on (optional)

All of these tools can be replaced with anything that feels meaningful to you and right for your ritual purposes. In general, for a casting a more elaborate circle, you will want to place an abject, or multiple objects in the spaces of the 4 cardinal directions. As you call each direction into your circle you can place the items in their designated point of the circle, opening yourself and your magic to an even greater power.

An example would be laying your athame at the South point of your circle and lighting a candle or two, before stepping to the West with your chalice and/or dish of water.

You may choose to use a compass initially, but as you get better at practicing in your own space, you will always know where North is.

Some witches will lay stones and crystals around the circle, between each cardinal direction, to make an even more powerful energetic force field. You can also use salt, as long as you are okay with sweeping it up after you close your circle. Pouring salt in the round is a fine way to offer protection to your energy and build upon your circle. You can even use this tool in your Basic Circle Casting Ritual and just cast your circle using salt only, speaking the names of the directions and asking for protection.

If you need a chair or a pillow to sit on for your spell work and rituals, you will want to make sure they are inside of your circle before you cast. Additionally, make sure all of the tools you need are inside the circle before you cast. You don't want to have to break the circle in order to run to your kitchen and grab some herbs. Be prepared and set it up accordingly with all of the ingredients and tools you will need to practice your magic.

Step 3: How to Open

1. Stand in the center of where your circle is going to be and inhale deeply and exhale fully, three times. This is a grounding act to get you focused and open to the energy of intentions for casting. It is essentially a meditation to prepare you for magic.

2. You can use a wand, or your pointer finger instead, to point at the place on the floor where you know the North to be and at the size you need your circle to be (ex: if you are making a bigger circle, you will need to point farther away from yourself to that point of the North).

   **NOTE: Some Wiccans start with the East and make the North position their last to call into the circle. It is really up to you whether you start with North or end with it, depending on your personal practices.*

   As you point to the North, imagine a figure of protection. It can be a deity, or even just a hooded warrior, or cloaked figure, who will bring light energy and protection. See them as your guardian of the North. Bow your head to them and acknowledge their arrival. Use a few words to ask for their protection, like: *"I call upon the Guardian and Protector of the North and the element of Earth to watch over this circle of magic."*

You may also choose to set your Northern objects and tools in this placement now, or you can set them up ahead of time, if you already want the cardinal directions of your circle to be ready before you stand in the center and take your three deep breaths from Step 1.

3. Keep your wand/ pointer finger outstretched and move to the next cardinal direction, moving counterclockwise, in this case it would be the East, if you are beginning with the North as your initial position. Repeat the steps from Step 2, to call upon a Guardian for the East. Picture their strength and what they represent, or see your god/goddess of choice for this direction.

4. Repeat this step for the South and the West, each time picturing your Guardian being and bowing your head in recognition after you speak words of invitation.

5. As you move fully through the circle and return to face the North, see in your mind the circle drawn on the floor, as well as the four guardians as towers of protection.

6. Point your wand (you can also clasp your hands together and point both of your index fingers into the air, calling

upon the great spirit, god/goddess, deity, or Earth Mother to join you and protect you from above and around in your circle.

**NOTE*: Before you begin, you can also set up a circle of salt on the floor to make it clear where your circle is going to lie as well as to add a greater level of protection. In addition to, or instead of salt, you can lay out your tools or elemental objects at each cardinal point, and add some stones and crystals all around the edges of the circle to outline the physical space you are wanting to work inside of. Doing this step before you stand in the center and begin your incantations to call the directions can be a mush more organized way to establish your circle.*

You will find what way works best for you and improve upon it as you go, and with each time you perform a sacred ritual.

Step 4: How to Close

Like with a Basic Circle Casting, it is important to thank and release the energies that you have called upon for protection at the endo of your ritual. This can mean just doing a reverse circle, exactly as it was performed in the opening, only working backward in a counterclockwise direction.

You can begin where you ended in the opening, and if you are using deities, or images of guardians to protect your circle, then be sure to thank each one at each point of direction as you move backward through your circle.

As a final offering, you can connect to the fifth element of spirit and declare your thanks for their presence in your rituals.

You can get as creative as you like with all of your incantations and words of closure. If you have a candle lit for your southern position, this would be a good time to snuff it out.

Whatever tools you used to connect to the cardinal directions can be collected and replaced on your altar. Depending on what kind of rituals you are doing, you may want to cleanse your tools with incense or smudging at the end of the ritual. Pick up any crystals and stones and return them to their homes, and sweep up any herbs or salt.

Leave your altar clean and tidy until your next circle casting. So mote it be!

This step-by-step guide to casting a circle is a huge part of your essential Wicca Starter Kit. As you have read, this type of magic will repeat itself over and over again and so it is important that you get comfortable with casting your circle of protection, as basic or as intricate as it may be.

In the next chapter, you will receive some simple step-by-step guidelines to help you get a grasp on the tools and energies required for a basic ritual.

Chapter 5: Step by Step Guide to Rituals

Rituals take many forms and represent so many different things to a Wiccan, or any person devoting themselves to this kind of magic. Rituals have existed for as long as human beings have, even in their most Neolithic forms. The ritual is a cause to express intentions and devotions through the world of energy, elements and spiritual connection and as you will notice in your research, every culture throughout history incorporates some kind of ritual practice into their lives.

In Wicca, rituals are about connection to the divine, spells, crafting and honoring the deities and rhythms of life. They are specific to each practitioner or coven, and can be delivered in a wide range of experiences and formats.

In your Wicca Starter Kit, you will have the step-by step guide to performing a ritual. Keep in mind that each ritual must be altered and enhanced according to whatever magical purpose you are working with. There may be a lot of ingredients for you to choose from and work with and there could be a lot of steps and degrees, or levels, of practice that you have to go through. It really depends on your spell, and whatever steps you are creating through your Book of Shadows and your solitary practice.

If you are in a coven, or choosing to become a part of one, many of the rituals performed are already outlined. This book focuses more on the ritual practices involved for a solitary Wiccan.

Let's get started with these basic and simple guidelines to help you picture the process of your ritual work.

Step 1: Preparations

Before any ritual begins, you need to make the proper preparations for it. Preparations can include all, or some of the following:

- Scheduling the ritual (Esbats and Sabbats have specific dates. Other rituals may need to fall on a certain date because of numerology, moon and sun cycles, birthdays, etc.)

- Organizing the steps (You will need to decide what order you need to carry out certain components of your ritual based on your own knowledge of a spell you are working, or referral to your Book of Shadows. Having the information handy and in your cast circle is an important part of preparing)

- Collecting your ingredients (You will need a variety of items, not including your altar or regular tools, that need to be used for your ritual. This can include specific herbs, crystals, candles and their colors, types of incense, etc.)

- Bringing all of your tools and ingredients into the space (You will need to have all of your collected tools, objects, ingredients spell book, or ritual instructions, and anything else you might need, in the space and ready to work on the chosen day and time)

- Setting boundaries with other life matters (You will need to turn off your cell phone and other distractions and create a time and a space with your family and loved ones to give you undisturbed time to practice your ritual)

You may find other preparations outside of what is on this list and that is all dependent upon the specific ritual or spell you are trying to cast.

Step 2: Casting Your Circle

For every ritual that you perform, for the sacred quality and nature of this experience, you will need to cast a Ritual Circle to support the energies you are trying to engage with and focus on.

Follow the steps for Ritual Circle Casting in Chapter 4 to prepare your circle of protection. Make sure that all of your tools, ingredients and objects needed for your ritual are already inside of the area you will be working in after your circle is cast.

Step 3: Honoring the Gods/Goddesses

Part of the reason people perform a ritual is to honor a sacred deity to their practice. Many Wiccans perform rituals for a specific God or Goddess and honor them regularly through a ritual to help them enforce their energies to work on other magical purposes.

The honoring of a deity or spiritual presence through a ritual is a sacred way to incorporate that presence int your everyday Wicca practice and will help bond you more deeply to the kind of magic you are choosing to practice.

Rituals open your space and your energy to receiving more of the gifts of that divine presence and so after you connect to casting your circle off protection, you begin your words of blessing and prayer to the god or goddess you are calling into your ritual, either to honor them directly as the purpose for the ritual, or to include them in whatever other ritual you are working to perform.

Step 4: Tools and Ingredients

At this point in your ritual, you will likely need any tools and ingredients required to perform your ritual. You may have already used some of your tools during the casting of your circle and you will want to be sure to keep the tools you need to use in your ritual instead of using them for placement of the circle. For example, rather than place your Chalice of water in the west, place a bowl of water there and keep your chalice in the center with you, or on the altar so that you can use it for your ritual.

Whatever herbs and ingredients you need to use can be prepared in whatever fashion they need to be. There are going to be specific instructions according to each ritual or spell and so you will need to have those instructions in the circle with you, to prepare your herbs and essences accordingly.

You will most likely be using your tools and ingredients together to compliment each other's energy. This preparation stage can be on your altar or on a table or on the floor where you are sitting.

Step 5: Connecting Your Intentions and Invoking Your Purpose

With your tools and ingredients ready to perform magic, you can begin the part of the ritual in which you will charge your tools and ingredients with the intentions and purposes of the ritual you are performing. You have read in Chapter 3 about how to charge and consecrate your tools.

Depending on your spell work and your intentions, you will imbue your ingredients, objects and tools with that sacred purpose at this stage to prepare for the rest of the ritual. Putting that magical intention into your objects and tools first, will only empower your ritual more fully and is an important step in the process.

Be specific and clear and let your intentions and magical purposes invoke the appropriate energy for your ritual.

Step 6: Practicing Magic

With your tools, implements and ingredients charged and consecrated, you can now begin to practice your ritual magic. This stage will include a wide variety of steps and is entirely dependent on what your Book of shadows says to do, or whatever your spell work instructions might ask of you. Some of these steps can include:

- Lighting the candles specific to your spell (they will already be charged, consecrated and anointed if you followed the last step)

- Burning of certain herbs

- Using your tools in a specific way to invoke and honor specific energies and/or deities.

- Dancing

- Chanting

- Speaking Spell words

- Pouring specific beverages into the chalice to drink and honor a deity or holiday celebration

- Appointing certain elements to aid and guide you through the use of your wand or athame.

- Burning ingredients in your cauldron

There are plenty of other possibilities that will arise with certain rituals and spells. Some, none, or all of these things can occur on your ritual and it will be up to your Book of Shadows and your intuition to build the ritual and the steps involved.

Step 7: The Power of Words

This step will really overlap inside of Step 6, as the words that you use for practicing magic will have a powerful impact on your ritual. You may say words during your ritual crafting and spells, but you may also have words to say after to really empower and solidify your intentions and purposes.

Your words are specific to what you are celebrating and can be as simple or as elaborate as you choose. A sample of some words for a basic spell honoring the Triple Goddess on a Full moon ritual might be as follows:

Triple Goddess of the Moon, I honor thee with the power of three. [light three candles, one for each aspect of the Goddess, as you speak the following lines]

Maiden sweet of springtime moon, I light this candle to honor you. [light the maiden candle]

Mother full of summer moon, I light this candle to honor you. [light the mother candle]

Crone in depth of darker moon, I light this candle to honor you. [light the crone candle]

Sacred Goddess throughout the year, on this full moon, I honor you here. [light your Triple Goddess herbs with fire to burn in your cauldron]

84

Bring to me your power of life, birth-death-rebirth, on full moon's light. [pour wine, water, or another beverage into your chalice]

I drink to thee, by power of three, to honor your sacred wisdom. [take three sips from the chalice, one for each aspect of the Goddess, with the next three lines]

To the maiden [sip]

To the mother [sip]

To the crone [sip]

By this full moon, I honor your vision.

So mote it be!

Wicca is a creative practice and a poetry of magical intention. Your words can be designed by your own power and so anything you choose will specifically empower your spells and rituals to help you access deeper wisdom and scared connection to the great divine.

Plan out what words you will say prior to your ritual and have them available to read if you do not know them by heart.

Step 8: Closing Your Circle

Once you have performed all of the steps included in your ritual, you begin to close the circle. Use the same steps you learned in Chapter 4 about how to close your circle and let your intentions carry forward into your life after your closing practice.

You may choose to decorate your altar with any of your ritual ingredients and you will want to organize your tools back on your altar so they can be ready for the next ritual you are planning.

After the Ritual

After your ritual, having returned your tools and ingredients and closed your circle, you can now work with the energies you have called upon to help you on your path of magic. Your altar serves as a reminder to you what rituals you have performed and why, keeping your intentions alive and your focus pure.

The energy of your ritual will only last for so long, and so you will need to decide when to move forward, clearing your altar of any remaining components of your last ritual practice. You want to keep your energy flowing, as is with all natural rhythms in life.

Use your intuition to know when the powerful energy of your ritual has waned and when it is time to send that ritual forward into the next plane of spirit. You will know the more your practice and tap into your own inner guidance as you perform more magic throughout your practice.

Chapter 6: Step by Step Guide to Spell Craft and Basic Spells

There is an endless collection of spells to be found online, in books, and through your friendships and relationships with other witches. There is an entire industry of spell books available and people are working to expose more and more options for crafting spells to make it all more accessible to the practicing witch or Wiccan.

There really isn't any reason not use someone else's spells, however this book allows for a more creative approach and honors the gift of crafting your own spells for your own specific purposes. Spells evolve and change, just like you do and it is okay to play around and get creative.

There are a few simple guidelines and step-by-step instructions to help you write and organize your own spells. This chapter will give you the outline you need to get started in creating your own Book of Shadows by practicing your own creative magic and spell writing work.

Step-by-Step Guide to Writing Your Own Spells

Step 1: Determine Your Goal, Intention, or Magical Purpose

Quite possibly the most important step in designing your spell, the goal or purpose is what will help you structure everything about your spell. What are you wanting to accomplish? Are you looking for love? Are you trying to draw more financial abundance or prosperity into your life? Are you wanting to honor a specific deity?

There are a lot of possibilities and they all require a specific intention. Be clear. Be direct. Keep it simple. Know what it is you are trying to magically manifest in a very honest and direct format so you can build and create your spell around that goal.

Step 2: Determine What You Will Need to Achieve Your Intention

Spells need tools and ingredients, although some might need only a candle or a crystal. Whatever you are going to need, you will need to decide your list of ingredients for your recipe. Some of the ingredients will come from the following list and all of them should be goal-specific according to your intention for the spell:

- Colorful candles
- Incense
- Herbs
- Objects from Nature
- Crystals and/or stones
- Altar Tools
- Bowls, containers, mixing spoons (all consecrated for rituals)
- Special garments
- Indoor or Outdoor set up/ altar (spell specific)

You may find even more items that you will need than what is listed here and you can always add things to every spell that you create based on what kind of Wicca you are practicing and what kind of spell you are casting.

Step 3: Determine the Timing

Every spell has a different energy that needs to guide it. Your spell may need to fall on a specific date, or even at a specific time of day. You may need the full sun, shining down on your spell, or you may need the darkness and energy of a New Moon.

Every spell has a time to make it work, and that time could also be anytime. Some spells will be open to work whenever you are needing them to be performed and the results may be different for you, depending on your approach.

Many Wiccans will cast their spells in accordance with what moon, or seasonal cycle they are in, in order to help the power of the spell feel enhanced or to generate a greater manifestation possibility.

Whatever time you decide to work your spell is important to the nature of your original goal. Choose the timing based on your intentions. If you are trying to grow your money and security, you may want to cast your spell on a New Moon and watch your money grow as the Full Moon grows, too. You may need the energy of the dawn hours to bring a powerful focused day and work experience into fruition, as a fresh start from the morning sunlight.

All of your spells can be written in the Book of Shadows you are building and it is helpful to give yourself feedback on the most powerful times to perform each spell. You may need to play around with the timing for each spell, if you are repeating them, so that you can hone in on the timing that manifests the greatest return for you.

Step 4: Decide on Your Words and Incantations

As you learned from the Step-by-Step Guide for Rituals in the last chapter, your words are important. They carry the meaning of your goal in to the energy of the Universe to help make it manifest, so you want to make sure that you are clear in your wording and meaning.

Writing your spell is a big part of the process and should always be done beforehand and not after you have cast your circle. If you want your spell to work, you need to find the right words for your goal.

The world of magic isn't sinister, but it can have a sense of humor as to how you receive your rewards and gifts from your spell work. 'Be careful what you wish for' is a popular saying, and in spell casting, that couldn't be truer.

Make sure you know what you are asking for before you set your intentions. It will likely come back to you.

Step 5: Organize the Spell into a Workable Format

Once you have determined all of the elements from Steps 1-4, you are now ready to construct the spell. They are the puzzle pieces and now you have to put the puzzle together. This part can be the most fun as it is the design phase of your spell.

Here is where you get to be the architect and determine what happens first, next and last. You will decide when to light the ritual candles you have chosen, and what words you will say alongside the sacred act of lighting them. You will decide exactly what method you will take to incorporate your herbs (burning, drinking as tea, displaying at the altar, wrapping for drying purposes, etc.). You will decide when to speak the words of manifestation in conjunction with each sacred and magical act.

Building the spell is part of the work you will incorporate into your Book of Shadows. It acts as a journal of your writing spells and your progress with them, so don't be afraid if you have to scribble things out and change some elements and factors. It is an ever-evolving work of art, just like every spell you create and every piece of magic you perform.

Step 6: Use Your Spells

After you have created your spell, the best part is using it. You will want to make time and space and collect all of your ingredients to have fun with your work of magic art. Using your spells is the pay off and the reward and your goals and intentions are set into motion every time you use them.

The next section will offer some basic spells to give you a place to start and familiarize yourself with some basic spell examples.

Don't hesitate to borrow these spells and change them to your liking.

Basic Spells to Help You Practice

Spell of Abundance

You will need:

- Copper bowl (if you can't find one, you can supplement the solid copper for another metal, like a silver goblet or chalice)
- Three gold coins
- Fresh spring water (you can also collect water from nature- a river or a waterfall, or a natural spring if you know of one in your area)

Instructions:

1. Plan to use the power of the Full Moon for this spell; schedule accordingly.

2. Create sacred space at your altar, using only candle light at night to perform your spell. If possible, perform close

to a window so that you can receive the full moon light coming in the window. You can also perform this ritual outside to get closer to the Full Moon energy.

3. Make sure your space is calm and that you are alone and undisturbed.

4. Fill the copper bowl half way with the spring water.

5. Cast a Circle

6. Toss the gold coins in, one at a time.

7. Find the reflection of the moon in the water inside of the bowl.

8. Focus on the reflection and state the following words:

"I ask that abundance flow into my life.
I awaken my riches by Full Moon's light.
My intention is prosperity
And my gratitude will last from here to eternity."

9. Close your circle.

10. Leave the bowl overnight. You can leave it under the Full Moon if you desire, or keep it on your altar.

11. In the morning, take the coins and put them in your purse or wallet, careful not to spend them.

**NOTE: *You can add some herbs and other tools, like anointed candles that represent money and abundance to keep safely lit overnight with your bowl of coins.*

Law of Attraction Spell

What do you need to attract the most of in your life? Love? Happiness? Wealth? Promotion at work? Psychic vision? Use this spell as a multi-purpose attraction for whatever your specific intention is. It is a spell to help you empower your energy to open to what you are truly wanting.

You will need:

- Two candles (color specific to intention)
- Paper and pen (you can use colored pens to enhance your intention)
- Cauldron
- Matches/ lighter

1. You can use your altar space, or another area where you can focus and be undisturbed.

2. Make sure you are in the right mind space to work this spell. Any negative or doubtful feelings that you may have will have a negative impact on the energy of your spell.

3. Cast a Basic Circle

4. Write your intentions on the paper. Be specific and clear.

5. Light your candles.

6. Read your intentions out loud if you like.

7. Catch the paper on fire with the flame of both candles.

8. Place the paper in your cauldron to safely burn.

9. While it burns, repeat the following words as many times as you can before the paper burns completely:

   "Let me be seen, heard and blessed on this day, harming no one on my way."

10. Close your circle before the next step.

11. Take your cauldron outside and feed the ashes to the wind if there is any to blow the ashes, or let them fall from the cauldron and waft into the air.

12. Instead of blowing out your candles, leave them burning or snuff them out.

13. Repeat this spell up to nine consecutive nights to help enhance the power.

14. If you aren't seeing any results, clear your energy and intentions and try again after about a month.

Herbal Love Charm Spell

This spell is a charm to help you release your blocks to love so you can attract it into your life better. A combination of herbs made into a sachet as a charm is a perfect way to enhance your openness to love. If you can't get all of the herbs on the list, that's okay! Just work with what you are able to find.

You will need:

- 5-8 whole cloves
- 1 tsp mugwort (dried)
- 1 tsp lemon balm (dried or fresh)
- 1 tsp St. John's wort (dried)
- 1/3 cup chamomile flowers (dried)
- 3 tbsps rose petals (dried or fresh)
- bowl
- 1 pink candle
- Square piece of cloth and string to tie into a sachet (like a potpourri bag)

Instructions:

1. Cast a Circle (basic or ritual)

2. Have your ingredients ready to work with on your altar.

3. Light your candle as you take deep breaths and consider your intentions.

4. Mix the chamomile, mugwort, lemon balm and St. John's wort with your fingers in the bowl.

5. Pour onto the cloth.

6. Sprinkle in the rose petals and cloves.

7. Close the sachet with the string

8. Hold the love charm in your hands in front of the candle and see your whole body covered inside and out with white light. Imagine it pouring out of your heart and filling your whole being. It can even fill the whole circle you have cast.

9. Now let sweet, pink light come from your heart and pour into the white light, as you hold your charm.

10. Say the following phrase, or whatever feels right to you, three times:

"With this charm of loving herbs,
My blocks to love I will disturb,
To remove them from my life,
Waking love and bringing light."

Play around with the words to find the right meaning for yourself. The spell is about releasing unwanted block to let love flow through you freely and accept it openly.

11. Let the candle burn out of its own accord (make sure it is in a safe space to burn at length).

12. Close your circle.

13. Wear your charm and keep it near you as often as you can. Sleep with it under your pillow even.

14. When the charm has fulfilled its magic purpose, you can bury it in the Earth, and/or, sprinkle the herbs somewhere, like in a flowing river to let your love continue to flow or grow.

Chapter 7: Step by Step guide to Crystal Magic

Crystals are one of the most popular tools for exchanging and enhancing energy. They are very useful to carry around on your person, hold in your hand, or wear as jewelry. For most Wiccans, the use of crystals and stones is a regular practice because of how strong their energy naturally is and how easy it is for them to absorb the kind of energy you want to carry with you after you charge and consecrate them.

There are a significant number of crystals and stones that can be acquired for use in your rituals and when you are making use of these tools, they will follow the same basic principles as with your other tools:

- They need to be cleansed regularly.
- They can be charged and consecrated as often as you need.
- They will hold unwanted energy after a time, so develop a relationship and intuition with these tools.
- Keep them in sacred spaces and respect their energy and magic.

If you already have some of your own stones, you may be familiar with how they each have a unique personality and quality. There are a variety of stones that are specifically for protection and others that are for attracting abundance and prosperity. You will find some that are for grounding and others that are best for opening clear channels of communication with your life or with the divine.

Here are just a few of some of the crystals and stones you may be working with to help you with your solitary practice:

Amethyst: purple crystal- self-discipline, pride, sobriety, inner strength, calms fears or anxieties, opens dreams and psychic visions, clear channel for communication with spirit, helps break habits and addictions.

Black Tourmaline: cleanses auras, breaks obsessions, heals anxiety, repels negativity, prevents psychic attack on the spiritual plane. Protective, grounding shielding.

Black Onyx: hard, black stone- banishing and releasing. Wards of negativity and conflict. Protection stone. Boosts confidence and strength.

Blue Kyanite: crystalline-blue stone- balancing, promotes clear personal truth, new chapters, clears auras and chakras. Doesn't need to be cleansed or purified, like other stones.

Carnelian: bright orange stone-, passion, determination, courage, motivation and individuality, success, inner fire, goal-manifestation, productivity, directness, joy, warmth, illumination.

Citrine: sunny yellow crystal- sun energy, joy warmth, friendship, communication, dream manifestation, individuality.

Hematite: strongly magnetic- all kinds of attraction magic, protection, stability, grounding, clear understanding and perspective.

Lapis Lazuli: deep blue with flecks of shining pyrite- openness, insight, truth, inner power, spiritual universal truth, interpretation of intuitive thought, psychic ability, soul guide magic.

Moonstone: milky white/grey- moon magic, intuition, life cycles, empathy and clairvoyance, emotional love, connections of the heart, empathy and kindness.

Quartz Crystal: clear and glassy- all-purpose energy stone, personal power and energy, clearing, balance, healing, spiritual growth and enlightenment, amplifies intentions.

Rose Quartz: soft pale pink stone- compassion, tolerance, love, peace, reveals inner beauty, self-confidence booster, relationships, self-love.

Tiger's Eye: warm golden brown-courage, willpower, loyalty, truth, luck, protection, truth-seeking, perception, cuts through illusions, brings to light manipulative or dishonest intentions.

Turquoise: bright blue with dark veining- master healer stone, inner beauty, joy, relaxation, healing, contentment, positive vibrations, prosperity, joy, friendship, protection, neutralize negativity, empath stone.

Step-by-Step Instructions for Crystal Magic

As with all of the information you have learned in this Wicca Starter Kit, your intentions and your energy are what cast magic. With all of the tools that you have found in your tool kit, you are now able to charge and consecrate them, as well as use them for specific spells and rituals.

Crystals have so many uses and you will discover more and more of what they can do and how they can improve and enhance your magic spells.

These basic step-by-step instructions are a guide to show you haw to care for and use your crystals and stones. They will work for you if you take good care of their energy.

Step 1: Clear and Charge

The first step with all crystals is to make sure they are cleared first. They are very absorbent and can hold onto a lot of energy, more than might be obvious when you are holding it in your hands.

In Chapter 3: Step 3, you can find the step by step instructions for clearing your crystals and stones. The same rules apply to all of your tools and your crystals are no exception.

Whether you are using salt, soil, sunlight, moonlight, or smoke. Regular clearing of your stones is very important to the magic you work with.

Charging your stones is the next best thing you can do. These steps are also listed in Chapter 3: Step 3, and you can use any means you think appropriate for charging. The key to a simple charging of the stones and crystals is to use your energy to imbue them with your powerful essence and magic. Set the intentions of wanting your stones to be clear, full of loving light, and charged by the power of whatever source you are inclined to choose: sun, moon, fire, smoke, etc.

Step 2: Cast the Magic

With your new knowledge of rituals and spell casting from chapters 5 and 6, you have all of the steps you need to cast the right kind of magic with your stones. Once your stones are charged, you can cast a spell with them and keep them energetically present within the work of the spell.

You may leave them on the altar or may carry them with you on your person. The casting of the magic is the moment in which you clarify your intentions and magical purpose into the stone. The crystals absorb the magical intention and are then full of your purpose and needs.

Consider this worthy of casting a basic or ritual circle and creating a spell specific to using your crystals so that you can really put the power and force of your spell work into these strong conduits of energy and spirit.

Step 3: Access Energy of the Crystals

Once your spell is complete, you can make use of the energy captured in the crystal and carry it with you. Depending on your needs and uses, you may be using your stone to protect your car and will leave it on the dashboard; you may be encouraging your garden to grow healthy and full and so you will be planting several of them in your garden bed; you may need it under your pillow to induce lucid dreams.

Whatever the spell is calling for you will need to now access the power of the magic encapsulated in your crystal and call upon it regularly in order to manifest your magic work.

Step 4: Clear and Charge

At some point, your spell will lose power and force, as will the energy in the stone. Once you have reaped the benefits of your crystal spell, you will then resort back to the first step by clearing and charging your crystal again, for its next magical use.

If you are working with crystal magic, these steps are a must to make sure that you benefit the most from using the energy of crystals and stones. Have fun with it, and to get you started, here is a crystal spell:

Crystal Spell for Clear Communication

Use this spell to improve communication at home, in relationships, at work, or even with the divine, or favored deities.

Charging a stone or a crystal with your magical purpose and intention is a very powerful way to open yourself to that magic. Stones and crystals, as you have read, are very powerful and hold a lot of energy. This spell is a great way to infuse your stone or crystals with the power of your intentions. It is meant to be carried or worn on the person so that you can connect to the energy of that purpose throughout the day.

You will need:

- Aquamarine
- amethyst
- clear quartz (optional)
- 1 white or yellow candle (colors of communication)

Aquamarine is a bridge between the heart and throat chakra and therefore promotes a clear channel of heartfelt, honest, open and compassionate communication. This is a stone for speaking truth. You can also add a piece of lapis lazuli to enhance that power and carry both stones with you (optional).

Amethyst is notable for opening your sense to communications through the divine and spirit. It can clear energy blockages to help with the flow of energy, including communication.

Quartz can be used to enhance the overall power of your spell when used in conjunction with the other elements.

Instructions:

1. Cast a Basic Circle.

2. Place your amethyst (and quartz) in front of your candle and light it.

3. Hold your aquamarine (and additional stones if using) in both your hands, palms pressed together.

4. Close your eyes and ground yourself. Take several deep breaths.

5. Spend time visualizing your communication moment and the feeling of relief and satisfaction as the result of your clear and direct communication. Picture yourself calmly and openly talking truth and how good it feels to express yourself.

6. Picture that energy flowing from you through your hands and into the stone.

7. Speak the following words while holding the stones in your hand:

    My voice is true and clear, of heart.
    I give these stones my powerful start,

To use my voice as clear as a bell,

I speak my truth and all I have to tell."

And so it is!

**NOTE: If you are wanting to communicate more with the divine than a family member or boss, you can change the words spoken to reflect that purpose and intention.

8. Now, place the aquamarine (and/or other stones) next to the amethyst and quartz and let the candle burn there for at least an hour or until burned out.

9. Close your circle.

10. You can now carry your stone with you to give you the energy of clear communication in the moment when you need it the most.

**You can also add herbs and oils to your candle to incorporate some additional power and magic to this spell. Frankincense essential oil and dried peppermint would be an excellent way to derive more clear communication from your candle magic.

Chapter 8: Step by Step guide to Candle Magic

Candle Magic is easy and fun. A candle is one of the more important tools you will use in any of your spells. Not only does it represent the element of fire and the direction of the south, it also brings light to your altar and gives life force to your magic. It is the one tool in the tool kit that can represent all of the elements, as you read in chapter 2.

With candle magic, all you need to know are a few basic things:

1. **Colors-** each color in the rainbow has meaning and magical purpose. The color of candle that you choose has a great impact on your spell. There are several meanings for each color and for some spells you may need a variety of colored candles to activate your magic. The color carries meaning as much as lighting the flame does.

2. **Symbols-** symbols are often carved into the wax of the candle in order to give it an additional power, purpose and meaning. Pentagrams or pentacles are rather common, but you may also have a lot of symbols that you already like to work with for your spells. Whatever the symbol, carving it into the candle and allowing it to melt away as the spell gains power is an important part of the ritual of candle magic.

3. **Oils-** oils rubbed on the sides of the candle add an additional essence to the magic. You may find that the added aroma can have a pungent impact and positive output for your spell. Many Wiccans use essential oils, or even herbal olive oils to anoint the candles for extra magical focus. This is usually a step that occurs before rubbing herbs onto it.

4. **Herbs-** herbs are heavily used in magic and they can even be helpful with consecrating your candles for heightened magical purposes. Using dried or fresh herbs adds the powerful property of whatever you are using to the power of your spell. You want the herbs to stick to the edges of the candle, so doing this step after you wet it with oils, is best.

Apply the above steps to your candle magic rituals and find an even greater resource of power in your craft work. Here is a list of some of the candle color meanings to help you with your spells:

White: all colors, innocence, the Maiden (Triple Goddess), purification, peace, healing, truth and sincerity, cleansing, spirituality, clarity, wholeness and joy, protection against negative energy, meditation, calm, focus.

Yellow: intellect, inspiration and creativity, communication, confidence and charm, persuasion, wisdom, mental strength, concentration, memory, logic and learning, personal power, self-esteem, cheerfulness, joy, optimism, Air element.

Orange: success joy, stimulation, energy, prosperity, good fortune, courage, energy building and boosting, power, legal matters happiness and enthusiasm, clears negative emotions, attracting friendships, emotional healing.

Pink: all forms of love, forgiveness, emotional and spiritual health, harmony, joy, compassion, love spells.

Red: fire and passion, fertility, sex, power, virility, potency, courage, blood, action, vigor, Mother (Triple Goddess), Fire element.

Purple: highly spiritual, psychic abilities, awakening, vision, clairvoyance, inner eye, intuition, respect, honor, wisdom, purification, progress, spiritual growth, stress reduction, insomnia, healing.

Blue: soothing, inner peace, harmony, tranquility, patience, kindness, healing, serenity, truth, wisdom, communication, loyalty, peaceful home, Water element.

Green: Mother Earth, fertility, nature, growth, abundance, financial success, money, luck, prosperity, generosity, emotional and physical healing/ rejuvenation, renewal, good harvest, earth magic, Earth element.

Brown: grounding, balance, earth vibration, clear thinking/ decision making, common sense, stability, material gain, concentration, intuition, telepathy, locating lost objects, animal healing.

Silver: neutralizes negative energies and influences, protection against entities, stabilizing, inner pace, serenity, invoking female deities.

Gold: solar gods and goddesses, attracting cosmic influences, wealth, persuasion, victory, masculine, confidence, invoking male deities.

Black: banishes negativity, absorbs all colors, reverses hexes/curses, repels black magic, rids of bad habits, resilience, self-control, inner strength, deeper consciousness, healing support with loss and grief, Crone (Triple Goddess).

Candle Spell for Money Flow

This money attraction spell is specifically geared towards candle magic. It is important while working this spell that you trust that your intentions will pay off, and that you don't need to worry about how it will happen. The Universe will deliver and you will have to stay open to any possibility.

You will need:

- One candle (gold or green for money spells)

- A candle holder or surface it can be stick to with melted wax (take safety precautions when working with candles)

- Sewing pin or crystal (the point of the pin or the point of a crystal will be used to inscribe a symbol into the candle)

- Patchouli essential oil (substitute olive oil if you have none)

- pinch dried basil

Patchouli and basil are herbs associated with wealth and money. You may come across other herbs that hold the same kind of magic and so you can decide on other herbs if you find something you like better.

Instructions:

1. Cast a Basic or Ritual Circle

2. Use the pin point or crystal point to inscribe a pentacle into the side of the candle (you can also choose other symbols that pertain to abundance, like runes or other ancient symbols you prefer)

3. Anoint the candle, rubbing the patchouli oil on the sides.

4. Roll the candle in the dried basil, allowing the herbs to stick to the patchouli oil on the candle.

5. Place your candle in its holder and make sure that the symbol you inscribed on it is facing you.

6. Take some time to ground yourself. Close your eyes and visualize that act of unexpectedly receiving money. You can also visualize yourself with paper money raining down on you, or standing in a river flowing with shiny coins and paper bills.

7. With the imagery focused in your mind, speak the following words, or something similar:

"With fire light I summon the divine forces,
Money flows to me from hidden sources.
Showering me with wanted gifts,
Surprising my pocketbook with a lift!"

8. Light the candle and as the wick sets to flame, announce: "So mote it be!"

9. Close your circle.

10. Leave the candle in place until it has burned out. Take safety precautions.

Conclusion

Congratulations! You are fully equipped with everything you need to get you started on your journey as a solitary practitioner to cast your spells and perform your rituals. This book is a wonderful resource for you to use again and again as you build your tool box of magical implements and practice creating your spells with everything you have to work with.

As you move forward, look back through these pages as needed to help you write your own spells and rituals and find the right methods for you to create space with your altar and your tools. Keep looking for more information to build upon your magical practice and find new tools and implements of your own unique and eccentric making or finding to add to rituals and tool box.

I hope that you have found this book useful and helpful and if you have, a review on Amazon.com is greatly appreciated. I leave you with the words to help you on your way, and may you find all of the magic that you need in these pages today!

As you move ahead on this path of light,

May it bring you great insight.

Casting magic, making bright,

Ritual spells by Full Moon Light.

Honor Goddess, Mother Earth,

Father Sky, as you give birth,

To all the magic of your heart,

May this book be your perfect start!

And so it is!

Made in the USA
Lexington, KY
22 September 2019